INSIGHT POCKET GUIDE

PHUKET

D0067780

Discovery CHANNEL

APA PUBLICATIONS

Part of the Langenscheidt Publishing Group

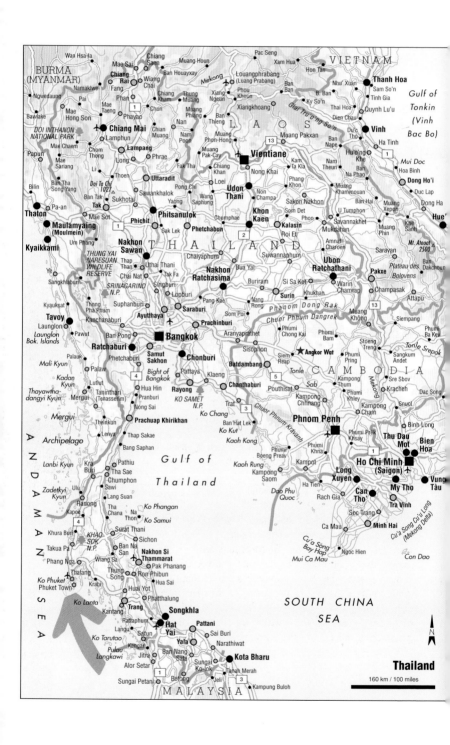

Thailand

160 km / 100 miles

Welcome

This guidebook combines the interests and enthusiasms of two of the world's best-known information providers: Insight Guides, who have set the standard for visual travel guides since 1970, and Discovery Channel, the world's premier source of non-fiction television programming. Its aim is to bring you the best of Phuket, Asia's premier beach resort, and its nearby islands, in a series of tailor-made itineraries devised by Insight's Thailand correspondent, Steve Van Beek.

White sandy beaches, warm aquamarine waters, balmy weather, an easy pace of life and sumptuous seafood are some of the attractions of this idyllic escape. Lesser known but just as attractive are its lush rainforest parks and the many nearby islands which offer spectacular scenery and some of the best reef diving in the world.

Van Beek has planned itineraries that cover not only the must-see sights but also the untrodden and quiet corners of this paradisiacal isle. This book captures the sunkissed attractions of Phuket with 10 full- and half-day itineraries. These cover everything from Buddhist temples and sea gypsy villages to rubber plantations and national parks – as well as the island's best beaches. And when you tire of Phuket's charms, there are six excursions further afield to yet more pristine islands and beaches, caves and rainforest reserves in its immediate environs. Complementing the itineraries are chapters on outdoor activities, shopping, eating out and nightlife, plus a useful practical information section detailing essential travel tips.

Steve Van Beek, a longtime resident of Thailand, has travelled the four corners of the country as both a travel writer and film director. Phuket will always remain special for Van Beek because he has watched it grow from a sleepy island backwater years ago to the international resort centre it is today. The island's attractions are manifold. 'In the unlikely event that you tire of its beaches,' says Van Beek, 'you will discover that the powdery white sands are only a nimbus between the blue-green sea and a rich interior.' Van Beek brings a keen insight and enthusiasm to this book, revealing places which are either largely ignored or glossed over quickly by other travel guides.

EXCURSIONS

Six excursions to destinations within easy reach.

LEISURE ACTIVITIES

CALENDAR OF EVENTS

PRACTICAL INFORMATION

MAPS

CREDITS AND INDEX

Pages 2/3: sunset at Kata Beach
Pages 8/9: fishing boats at Ko Phi Phi

History & Culture

The excitement of Phuket begins when you are still aloft, the plane floating over the deep green islands of Phang-Nga Bay and then over the farms and forests, and bays and beaches of the island. Before the plane banks for its final run from the emerald sea, you know you are about to touch down on an island that holds some of Asia's most spectacular scenery.

This aura is intensified by your first view of Phuket's beaches. Nudged by the breeze that blows off the Andaman Sea, the surf rolls in gently. Lacking the ferocious power of Atlantic breakers, the waves are not lions but lap dogs yapping at a sleepy ox of an island; or a benign sea god heaving himself ashore after a long swim. The surf's gentleness defines the pace of life along the palm-shaded, powdery sand beaches of Phuket. At the same time, it belies the island's turbulent history, a skeleton closet filled with explorers, pirates, empire builders, women warriors, sea gypsies and fortune hunters.

First Landfall

No historian can precisely pinpoint the origins of Phuket's early inhabitants. Hunters and gatherers lived in caves along the inner Andaman over 40,000 years ago when sea levels were low and it was possible to walk to the neighbouring Phi Phi islands. Historian H G Quaritch Wales believes that the first indigenous inhabitants were Semang pygmies and Moken sea gypsies. By the 3rd century AD, it is thought that Tamils from southeast India settled along the Andaman coast around nearby Takua Pa and Trang and set up a fledgling trade in commodities such as spices.

Written history first takes note of Phuket in the *Kedah Annals of Malaysia*, written around AD 1200. Its early mention in Malaysian literature is intriguing, since other than the Malay name bestowed on the island, Ujang Salang, there is no evidence that Malays inhabited it. Instead, archaeology suggests that the island was shared from an early date by Mon-Khmers from Burma, who occupied the northern region, and the Chao Lay (the latter word being short for *talay,* which means 'sea'), or sea gypsies, who built settlements along the southern coasts, most likely in the vicinity of Ko Sirey and Rawai.

Seventeenth-century European sailors followed crude maps to an island identified only as Junkseilon. It is thought that the name was a corruption of the Malay words 'Ujang Salang', which, when translated, mean 'northernmost island' or 'peninsula'. Because of the island's hilly landscape, the island was also given the appropriate Malay name of *bukit* or 'hill', a name that eventually became 'Phuket'.

Left: roof detail at Put Jaw Temple, Phuket Town
Right: Buddhist monk with his begging bowl

Phuket had an unsavoury reputation among 17th-century European sea captains who regularly logged complaints of pirates who preyed upon their ships along its shores. It is not certain if these pirates came from Phuket itself or elsewhere, but they attacked ships for their booty and Phuket villages for the slaves they could carry away to the Sumatran kingdom of Aceh.

By the 18th century, European ships were calling regularly at Phuket, using its calm bays to ride out storms. They also used the island as a replenishing source, obtaining prosaic items like fresh water, firewood and pitch to caulk their boats. Later explorers sought more valuable commodities, trading European products for ivory, gems and pearls. One of the treasures most sought was ambergris, the gray slime spewed by sperm whales and collected by fishermen. As the cloying agent in perfume, this cargo was prized in Europe, its value set ounce for ounce against the price of gold.

Today, Phuket has the second highest per capita income in Thailand, its key industries being tourism and rubber. Major crops are coconuts, rice, cashew nuts, cacao, tapioca and pineapples. Other earners are fishing, pearl cultivation and the harvesting of birds' nests. In 1974, only 16,000 tourists, mostly Malaysians, visited Phuket. By 2003, that number, comprising visitors from all over the world, had skyrocketed to more than 2.5 million.

In December 2004, massive waves caused by a powerful undersea earthquake off Sumatra devastated communities along Thailand's Andaman coast, including Phuket. The effects, thankfully, have been short-term and most businesses have since recovered.

Women Warriors

Although Phuket lies far from the centre of Thai royal power at Bangkok, it has played an important role in preserving the nation's sovereignty. The proximity of a rich island of strategic importance led the Burmese time and again to invade it. The most memorable battle occurred in 1785.

At that time, the capital was at Thalang in northcentral Phuket. The Burmese attacked from the sea, taking the island's defenders by surprise. The island's governor had just died, so the Thais were leaderless. Realising they were

outnumbered, Chan, the governor's widow, and her sister Mook, disguised the island's women as men. The great numbers of soldiers on the city's walls confused the Burmese, and the Thais' swift and harassing sorties on their flanks weakened them.

After one month, the Burmese decamped and sailed away. To honour the women for their bravery, King Rama I conferred royal titles on them. Chan became Thao Thep Kasattri and Mook, Thao Sisunthon. A statue on the highway from the airport portrays them standing and facing north, swords in hand and awaiting new invasions.

Phuket nearly played a prominent role in Western imperialistic aspirations in the 18th century. The British sought an island which could become the cornerstone of their empire in the Andaman Sea. Phuket seemed fit to serve as a port and a defensive bastion. Captain Francis Light, a merchant of the East India Company who had settled in Phuket and married a local woman, explored the possibilities of establishing a British base. In the end, bowing in part to suzerainty claimed by the Thai royal court in Bangkok, the British decided upon Penang, which more effectively guarded the northern end of the Straits of Malacca and countered the powerful Aceh kingdom on the northern tip of Sumatra.

Phuket's Changing Fortunes

In the reign of King Rama II (1809–24), the Burmese returned. They wreaked such destruction that the islanders moved to Ka Poo on the mainland, a town later renamed Phang Nga. Later, when the threat abated, the villagers returned to establish a new town in the north called New Thalang, halfway between where Phuket Town and the airport now stand.

New Thalang's prominence was, however, short-lived. When tin was discovered in large quantities in the south, a third town, Phuket, rose to dominate the island's political and economic life within a few decades.

Phuket's history since then has been a story of tin, rubber and tourism. The discovery of tin resulted in a wave of migrants, principally Chinese, who came to work the tin mines. Phuket became a boom town with all the attendant problems. Dissatisfaction with working conditions and rivalry between two Chinese secret societies resulted in the Miners' Rebellion of 1876, in which pitched battles were fought between police and miners. Statues at Wat Chalong pay homage to the monk who healed broken bones as well as the rift, serving as a mediator between the parties to quell the rebellion.

Phuket Town changed dramatically after a huge fire destroyed most of the downtown area

Left: Burmese ship in a battle against the Thais
Above: Chan and Mook. **Right:** King Rama I

at the beginning of the 20th century. Leading the reconstruction was one of the most important men in Phuket's history, Governor Rasada Korsimbi. Serving from 1900 to 1920, he instituted many of the changes which transformed Phuket Town into a modern city. Most of the mansions modelled after Portuguese colonial homes date from this period, including the Standard Chartered Bank Building and the Thai Airways International Office.

If tin changed the face of the island, then the introduction of the first tin dredger in 1907 by Australian, Captain Edward Thomas Miles, transformed its coastline. With it, tin mining moved offshore. There are still open mines today, but most have been swallowed up by the jungle or transformed into farms. The dredgers, however, have left their scars along the eastern coastline.

Even so, in 1908, a missionary named John Carrington could still write that Phuket 'is a place where wild elephant, rhinoceros, tiger, water buffalo, cattle, monkeys, birds, and reptiles abound.' Following a worldwide slump in tin and rubber prices, tourism became the island's prime revenue earner. Though Phuket Town has grown considerably, it has retained much of its original charm.

Phuket's People

Phuket has a population of about 300,000. Most are Thais who migrated from the mainland, or descended from the Chinese who arrived to work the tin mines, Muslims of Malaysian extraction who arrived at an earlier date, and Chao Lay or sea gypsies. The Chao Lay, a nomadic people, traditionally travelled from cove to cove, staying until the shellfish and other resources were depleted. They then moved on, allowing the cove to re-establish its former ecological balance before returning to repeat the cycle.

Sea gypsies are said to have originated in the Andaman and Nicobar islands between Burma and India. They are generally darker skinned and heavier with curly black hair that may appear light brown in many of the children. Two of the three main ethnic groups of Chao Lay have taken up a land-based existence, going to sea only to fish. They live in small houses set on short stilts and covered with corrugated tin roofs. They speak their own language and follow their own animistic religion.

The dominance of the island by the original settlers and Chao Lay, was diluted by the arrival of the Thais from the mainland and by the Chinese

Above: Portuguese-inspired architecture at Phuket Town

labourers. Thais of Chinese descent, who now comprise 30 percent of the island's population, differ from those in Bangkok in that they came from the Fujian region of China. As elsewhere in Asia, they gravitated from menial to mercantile professions. Today, the Chinese are responsible for much of the trade and commerce in the city.

A large portion of Phuket's Thai community is Muslim. Their numbers have grown and they comprise about 30 percent of the island's population. Concentrated around Surin and a few other big villages, they work in rice fields and rubber plantations. Among Phuket Town's merchants are Sikhs and Hindus whose families have resided on the island for decades. Most have assimilated into Thai culture, speak the language and bear Thai names.

Language and Culture

Southerners speak a form of Thai often incomprehensible to those from other parts of Thailand. While the grammatical structure and most of the words are the same, the accent is so strong that it sounds like another language altogether. They also snip syllables from either end of words, speaking a shorthand form of Thai, for instance, saying *pai lat* instead of *pai talat* (go to the market) or *muek* instead of *plaa muek* (squid).

The culture of the south has been flavoured by contacts with Malaysia to produce a number of art forms distinctly different from those of Thailand's other regions. During your stay in Phuket, try to view one of the two most famous southern art forms, the *Manohra* and the *Nang Talung*.

The *Manohra* (or *Nora* as shortened by southern Thais) is a dance-drama based on an Indian tale. The heroine, Nora, is a heavenly bird who marries a human prince. She is forced to return to heaven and he travels there to find her. The story is told in the form of a slow, sinuous dance with the silent dancers dressed in elaborate bird costumes, relating the tale in stylized, graceful gestures while an off-stage chorus supplies the lyrics.

Nang Talung is a form of shadow puppet theatre. *Nang* means 'animal hide', from which the figures are cut. *Talung* refers to Pattalung, a town on the mainland where the art form originated. The puppets differ from their stiff northern cousins in that one arm can be moved by a thin bamboo rod. The puppets perform against a back-lit white cloth screen. The repertoire includes episodes from the *Ramakhien* – which has its origins in the Hindu *Ramayana* – the classic story of the god-king Rama whose beautiful wife, Sita, is abducted by the evil demon king, Tosakan, and only rescued after great hardship and battles.

As interesting as the performance is the carnival-like atmosphere that prevails. Except for short excerpts at the Thai Village culture show *(Itinerary 7)*, village performances are rare. If one is being presented, it is well worth attending. They are largely informal affairs, and you can walk in or out at any time without offending the performers.

Right: *Nang Talung* puppets silhouetted against a back-lit screen

Religion

Theravada Buddhism is the dominant religion and its most prominent reminders are the *wat* (temples) and the monks in their saffron robes. Tradition requires that every Buddhist male becomes a monk for a minimum of seven days to gain an understanding of his religion and to make merit so he will return as a more evolved being in the next life. Because this tradition does not extend to women, the male also makes merit for his mother and sisters.

Each day at dawn, monks walk through the villages and towns surrounding their temples, to receive rice and curries from Thais who wait in front of their houses. On *wan phra*, weekly holy days determined by the lunar calendar, Buddhists visit the temples to hear monks chant sermons from ancient Pali scriptures. Of the 29 temples in Phuket, Wat Phra Thong *(Itinerary 4)* and Wat Chalong *(Itinerary 8)* are the most important.

For Phuket's Chinese, Mahayana Buddhism and Taoism are inextricably intertwined. The Chinese Buddhist shrines satisfy spiritual needs but the older Taoism provides specific gods for specific purposes, a more satisfying form of insurance against the vicissitudes of daily life.

Most Thai Muslims belong to the Sunni denomination. Muslim men can be identified by their plaid or checkered sarongs, beards (worn by *haji*, or men who have made a pilgrimage to Mecca) and knitted or brocaded skull-caps. Muslim women generally wear flowered sarongs and cover their heads.

While the Christian community is very small, there is a significant community of Sikhs who have their own temple on Suthat Road (the northern extension of Montri Road) and Hindus, whose Phuket Thendayudapani Temple is just south of the Sikh Temple. Both temples are found in Phuket Town.

Thai Values

While Buddhism is the principal influence shaping the Thais' moral and social behaviour, they hold several other values that single them out. One is *sanuk,* a concept which translates roughly as 'fun'. Thais judge the value of an endeavour by the amount of *sanuk* it contains; anything not *sanuk* is not worth pursuing. The Buddhist ideal of avoiding suffering has led to the adoption of an attitude of *mai pen rai*. This is roughly translated as 'it doesn't matter' or 'no problem', accompanied by a shrug of the shoulders. The surprise is that despite this laid back attitude, the Thais are a dynamic people, as the rapid development of their country attests.

Thailand has had to struggle to maintain these values against the onslaught of modern-day materialism, but its people have acquired an equilibrium that is admirable. It is these traits – equanimity, art, a gentle culture – that have drawn visitors to their country for centuries.

Above: Wat Chalong is Phuket's most important Buddhist temple

HISTORY HIGHLIGHTS

8th–12th century: Thais migrate from China and Vietnam into northern Thailand.

1238: Thais, led by King Intradit, establish an independent nation based at Sukhothai.

1350: Ayutthaya, farther south on the Chao Phraya River, supplants Sukhothai as Thailand's capital.

1767: After repeated attempts, Burmese armies overrun Ayutthaya and destroy the city. The Thai army regroups at Thonburi and engages in 15 years of wars with the Burmese, Laotians and Vietnamese.

1782: The wars subside. General Chakri (Rama I) assumes the throne, establishing the Chakri dynasty. He moves his headquarters across the river to Bangkok.

1851–68: King Mongkut (Rama IV) ascends the throne, reforms the laws and sets Thailand on the path towards modernisation. He encourages contact with the West.

1868–1910: King Chulalongkorn (Rama V) continues his father's initiatives. He preserves the sovereignty of Thailand, the only Southeast Asian nation that escapes colonisation.

1910–25: King Vajiravudh (Rama VI) concentrates on modernising the country. Thailand sides with the Allies during World War I.

1925–35: Economic troubles compound King Prajadhipok's (Rama VII) problems. In 1932, a *coup d'etat* occurs and King Prajadhipok accepts a provisional constitution by which he 'ceases to rule but continues to reign'. Dismayed by quarrels in the new government, the king abdicates in 1935.

1935–46: Ananda Mahidol (Rama VIII) is named king but remains in Switzerland to complete his studies. The Japanese occupy Thailand during World War II. In 1946, King Ananda dies and is succeeded by his younger brother, Bhumibol Adulyadej.

1950–72: On 5 May 1950, Prince Bhumibol is crowned King (Rama IX). The 1950s is a time of turmoil, with many *coup d'etat* and a succession of military-backed governments. In the 1960s, Thailand experiences an economic boom as a result of investment generated by the US.

1973–90: A civil uprising topples a despised dictatorship and a democratic government is elected. A right-wing counter-coup in 1976 re-establishes military rule. A former general, popularly elected in 1988, is deposed in a bloodless military coup in 1990.

1992: A new Democratic government under Chuan Leekpai is elected.

1995–97: In July, the Chart Thai party is elected. Two weak, corrupt governments mismanage the economy. The Thai baht is devalued in July 1997 and Thailand enters a recession.

1998: A new, more open Constitution is voted in. Chuan Leekpai returns as Prime Minister. Thailand follows guidelines established by the International Monetary Fund to resuscitate its financial systems and economy.

1999–2000: The economy shows signs of recovery.

2001: Thaksin Shinawatra, leader of the Thai Rak Thai party, is elected prime minister.

2004: Waves of attacks in largely-Muslim south, resulting in the deaths of more than 320 people.

2004: Tsunamis generated by a 9.0-Richter earthquake off the coast of Sumatra cause much devastation along Thailand's Andaman coast.

2005: Thaksin Shinawatra's Thai Rak Thai party wins a landslide victory in the general elections.

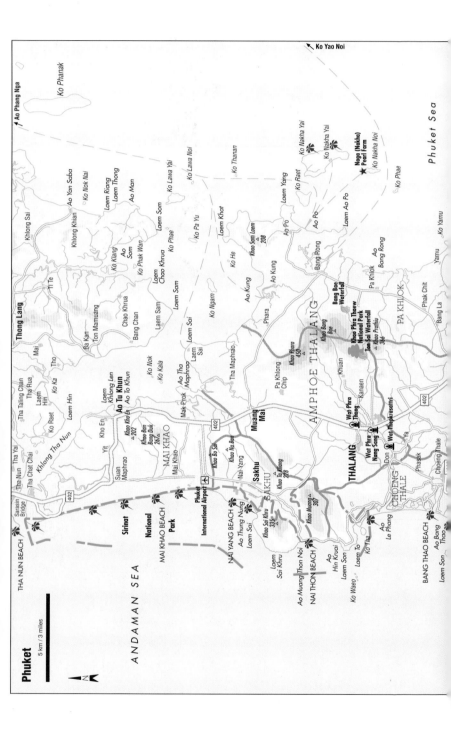

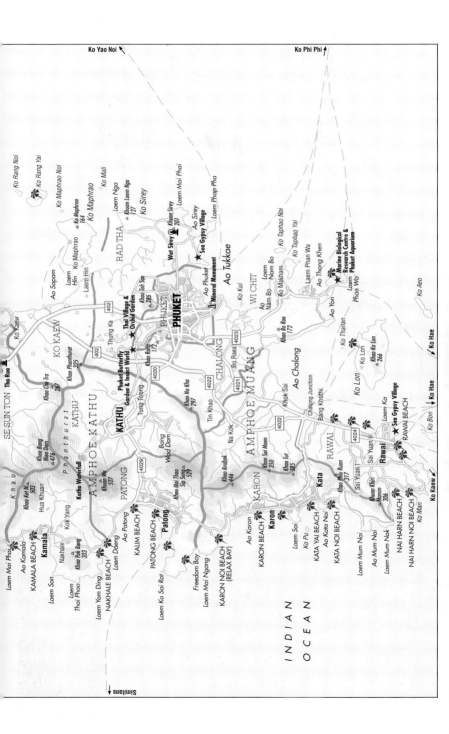

Island Itineraries

S pend your first two days exploring the beaches and Phuket Town. Later, head into the more remote areas, to discover why Phuket continues to be a magnet for travellers. These itineraries are designed to give you the widest possible latitude in exploring Phuket. Although the information is specific to each itinerary, you are encouraged to stray from the trodden path and make your own discoveries. Tourist establishments damaged by the December 2004 tsunami disaster have been restored, and most businesses are now back in operation.

Patong Beach has been selected as the starting point for the itineraries because it is where most visitors stay. If you stay at any of the other west coast beaches, just look at the maps provided in this guide and plan your trips accordingly. Patong is also the place where vehicles can be rented most easily, and cheaply. Most of the itineraries recommended here are best done by car, a four-wheel jeep, or motorcycle. Motorcycles are available from 90cc and up; a 125cc trail bike with good *dok yang* ('rubber flowers' or tread) is best. See *Practical Information* at the back of the book for more information on vehicle rental. You can use public transport, but service to distant destinations is infrequent or non-existent. Besides, public transport will not take you to all the sights described in this section.

Since most travellers visit Phuket to relax and enjoy the rare luxury of sleeping in, most journeys begin after a leisurely breakfast. It is certainly worth starting most of these itineraries in the morning, as the weather in Thailand after lunch can be extremely hot. While one hates to give up precious tanning time in order to traipse into the unknown, do it anyway. It will be worth prying yourself off the beach to discover some new sights.

The 'Chalong Junction', referred to in many of the itineraries, is the five-pointed star on the road to Rawai, and from which the roads to Rawai (H4024), Chalong and Kata (H4028), Phuket Town (H4021) and the bypass road (also designated H4021) radiate. For some reason, the number H4021 has been given to both the highway from Phuket Town to the Chalong Junction, as well as the road that bypasses the town to the west. Most roads in Phuket are narrow, but in reasonable condition. In this book, the word 'Highway' is sometimes abbreviated as 'H', while 'KM' refers to the kilometre post at the side of the road.

For those who wish to travel beyond Phuket island, the six excursions to places further afield will help you enjoy the stunning beauty of southern Thailand. All the destinations can be reached by boat, but you will probably find it more convenient to travel to Krabi *(Excursion 5)* by car, or flying there direct from Phuket.

Left: Buddha statue atop Khao Rang
Right: island signage

1. BEACH SAFARI *(see map, p24)*

It is the beautiful beaches, balmy air and warm sea that are Phuket's principal attractions, so spend the first day enjoying the beach that fronts your hotel. By the second or third day, you may want to know what lies over the next hill. The following is a brief description of Phuket's main beaches and their facilities.

To explore Phuket's varied beaches, it is best to rent a jeep along Patong Beach. Visiting all the beaches mentioned here will take a full day.

Phuket's beaches share the same powdery sand, blue-green water, casuarina and palm trees, and strutting mynah birds, yet each is unique and each satisfies a different kind of traveller. You may want to be a beach gypsy, changing accommodations from one bay to the next as you drive down the coast.

If you arrive on a morning flight, consider renting a jeep at the airport and driving around the island until you find a beach you like. This option, however, is not recommended during the high season when it is hard to find a room on *any* beach. Phuket's beaches line the western shore. The following are the key beaches, running from north to south.

Northern Beaches

With 9km (5½ miles) of snowy white sand, **Mai Khao** (White Wood) **Beach** is Phuket's longest. Its crystalline sands are devoid of litter and it is one of the island's few beaches that remain in a pristine state. The northern mangrove area and the former Nai Yang National Park further south are now preserved as the new **Sirinat National Park**. Dine at one of the small thatched restaurants on the northern end which serve excellent seafood at very low prices.

Between November and February each year, Mai Khao plays host to hundreds of Olive Ridley Sea Turtles, which come ashore each evening to lay their eggs. There have been sightings of the much larger Giant Leatherback Turtle coming ashore here, but recently these have been few and far between. Relatively new on the scene is the **J W Marriott Phuket Resort & Spa** at the northern end. A low-rise structure that blends in with the surroundings, this is the only hotel of note in this beautiful stretch of beach.

Fringed by a forest of tall casuarina trees, **Nai Yang Beach** is also part of Sirinat National Park and is thus secure against encroachment by unlicensed developers. Like Mai Khao, Nai Yang's beach is an important nesting site for Olive Ridley Sea Turtles. The Parks Department maintains several bungalows, which can be rented for 600–1,200 baht a night. Contact the Sirinat National Park Visitors' Centre (tel: 0 7632 8226).

If you are a keen snorkeller then swim out to the large coral reef nearly a kilometre from the shore. The comfortable **Pearl Village Resort** anchors

Above: this T-shirt says it all

the southern end. To reach Nai Yang from Mai Khao, return to Suan Maphrao town and take the Thepkasatri Road (H402) towards the airport for 10km (6 miles). Turn right onto H4026 and follow the signs for the Pearl Village Resort.

Leaving Nai Yang on the H4026 to the south, continue on to the village of Ban Sakhu. On entering the village take the small road to the right and follow the signs to the Nai Thon Beach Resort for 4km (2½ miles). **Nai Thon Beach** is one of the quietest on the island. It's sheltered from the wind by two large granite outcrops that protect the north and south of the bay. There are a number of small restaurants serving grilled seafood and local dishes. To the south of Nai Thon is **Hin Kruai Bay**, which rarely has a soul on it.

The coastal road continues south over Laem Son to **Bang Thao Beach**. Although Bang Thao is dominated by the Laguna Phuket resort development, which comprises five luxury hotels – including **The Banyan Tree** and **Sheraton Grande Laguna** – it is possible to find a quiet corner to swim. The bay is good for windsurfing as there is normally a gentle breeze blowing. The annual Phuket Laguna Triathlon is held here in December and usually attracts some excellent athletes from around the world.

From Bang Thao the road skirts various lagoons until it joins the H4025 just beyond the Choeng Thale village. Turning right, head towards the Muslim Bang Thao village and onto the next two beaches 3km (1¾ miles) away.

Pansea Beach has a beautiful cove anchored by huge boulders. Its pocket-sized beach, one of the very best on the island, is shared by expensive resorts like **The Chedi** and **Amanpuri** and is effectively off-limits to outsiders.

Surin Beach is one of those rare beaches that has yet to feel the hand of a developer but for good reason – from May to November the water can have a dangerous undertow. For the rest of the year, it's possible to swim here, but care must be taken at all times. If you enjoy seafood, why not try one of the small restaurants at the southern end of the beach. Many locals are drawn to these establishments and that's a sure sign of just how good (and cheap) they are.

Central Coast Beaches

Continuing south along the coastal road you will reach the beautiful **Kamala Beach**. The beach's setting is superb: a fishing village amidst coconut trees fronting its white sands. Like Surin, however, its bay is cursed by a bad undertow as both the beaches drop sharply into the water. The beautiful coral reefs lying slightly offshore are great for snorkelling and scuba diving, as the currents are not as strong when you move further away from the bay. However, be warned that this coast can be dangerous during the monsoon season. There are small, low-budget bungalows on the northern end, and several modern resort hotels at its southern end. The fishing village is a good place to sample Southern Thailand's famed Muslim cuisine (*Itinerary 9*).

Continue south on the coastal road for another 8km (5 miles) to arrive at Phuket's biggest and busiest beach

Right: top-up time

resort, **Patong Beach**. This 4-km (2½-mile) long, crescent beach, 15km (9 miles) west of Phuket Town, is the most developed of Phuket's beaches. It holds the widest array of water sports facilities, nightlife, shops and restaurants. Patong is, in short, for visitors who prefer a busy resort to a quiet, hidden beach. Patong also has Phuket's largest range of hotels.

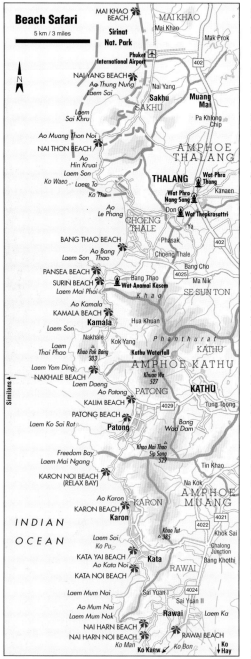

If searching for a hotel by perusing a brochure, be aware that hotel names in Patong often reveal more wishful thinking than truth: 'Bayshore' is separated by 150m (490ft) of concrete buildings from both the 'bay' and the 'shore'. And '150 metres beach front' could mean that it is 150m (490ft) from the beach, not exactly in a position to enjoy the gentle surf. When considering a hotel, check the ads carefully and ask questions. Among the better hotels found here are **Amari Coral Beach**, **Patong Merlin**, **Holiday Inn**, **Club Andaman Beach Resort** and **Impiana Phuket Cabana**.

A few kilometres south of busy Patong is **Tritang Bay**, home to the **Merlin Beach Resort**, followed by **Relax Bay**, with its single hotel **Le Meridien Phuket**. Nonetheless, like all beaches in Thailand, these are public too.

Just over Laem Khak lies **Karon Beach** and at more than 4km (2½ miles) in length, it is one of Phuket's longest beaches. Unfortunately, it is also one of its most treacherous during the monsoon season. On the other hand, during this same period of the year, Karon can be great for surfing. Morning glories cover a sandy ridge separating the beach from the back areas, giving some privacy and shelter from the noise of passing cars. The southern end of the beach is quite built up with a number of hotels and restaurants. Note: like Patong, the hotels in Karon are separated from the beach by a road.

Right: the Kata Thani Resort sits on prime beach front

The next two towns of Ban Karon and Ban Kata almost blend into one another. **Club Med** chose **Kata Yai Beach** for its second resort in Asia – and for good reason – it is spectacularly lovely. If you are a reasonably strong swimmer, the small offshore island of **Ko Pu**, which dominates the bay, is worth the swim. The relatively shallow waters of the bay make it one of the best beaches on the island for snorkelling. **Mom Tri's Boathouse** is the other hotel of note here.

Continuing south through Kata town, turn right into its spectacular beach-front. An idyllic setting, the southern end of **Kata Noi Beach** offers decent snorkelling. The sprawling **Kata Thani Resort** is the main hotel here. Nestled atop a rocky, forested promontory between Kata and Kata Noi, **Mom Tri's Villa Royale** occupies the former home of one of Thailand's most well-known architects and offers the best accommodation in Kata.

The Southern Coast

To reach the southern extremities of Phuket, you'll need to retrace your route back up the hill from Kata Noi and at the top, turn right and follow the signs to the 'Viewpoint'. From this point there's a splendid view of Karon, Kata Yai and Kata Noi beaches, all strung out before you. The road then swings inland, running through rubber plantations and pretty rice paddies.

Eventually, after some 4km (2½ miles), you will reach one of the loveliest beaches on the island, **Nai Harn Beach**, which lies between two ridges and faces the setting sun. Behind it is the beautiful lagoon that gives it its name. Offshore is **Ko Kaew Yai** island. **Le Royal Meridien Phuket Yacht Club**, situated at the northern end of the beach, is one of the island's premier hotels, with very good Thai and Italian restaurants.

From Nai Harn follow the road (H4233) around the beautiful Promthep headland and on to Phuket's southernmost tip, **Rawai Beach**. Here, the rocky foreshore at low tide is a magnet for shell collectors. Thirty minutes offshore are the coral islands of **Ko Bon** and **Ko Hae**. At the eastern end of the beach are some small seafood restaurants, a good place to take a break. The main hotel on Rawai is the spa-oriented **Evason Phuket**.

2. PHUKET TOWN *(see map, p28)*

An early morning walk through Phuket Town's streets to see a market, assorted Chinese temples, old colonial-style mansions, and the heart of the former Chinese quarter; continue south to visit an aquarium.

To get to the start point, take a bus or a tuk-tuk to Phuket Town's market on Ranong Road. If taking a tuk-tuk, remember to negotiate the rate in advance. This walking tour, without the aquarium visit, will take about 2 hours.

If you have arrived early, why not try a local breakfast before beginning your walk. At one of the tables along the pavement, dine on *khanom chin*, rice noodles buried under minced meat curry, or strong Thai coffee and crispy *patongkoh*, delicious deep-fried pastries.

Wander through the market, which sells fresh fruits and vegetables harvested from nearby market gardens. Sniff the air for the pungent scents of Asia: chillies, maroon mounds of pungent *kapi* (shrimp paste), betel nuts, pickled garlic and tamarind. Watch Thai housewives as they bargain and cajole the merchants and exchange gossip. Although it is mainly a fresh

produce market, it is possible to find good local clothing, including sandals, sarongs and northern Thai-style baggy trousers made of cotton.

Next, cross Ranong Road and walk to the left past the **Thai Airways International office**. Peek at the beautiful old colonial house at the rear of the compound. Continue up Ranong past Wat Nua, a Thai temple; along the wall is a lovely old wooden dormitory for monks.

Top: trishaw rider takes a break in front of the Phuket Town market
Above: market colour

Fortune Telling at Put Jaw Temple

At the next corner, cross the road to visit **Put Jaw Temple**. This Chinese Taoist temple is the oldest in Phuket and is dedicated to Phra Mae Koan-Im (Kuan Yin), the Goddess of Mercy. The original, built 200 years ago, was renovated about a century after it was first built.

The main hall holds statues of the goddess and her attendants. On the floor before the image is a can of what looks like shaved bamboo chopsticks. Shake the can back and forth rhythmically until one of the sticks works its way to the top and falls to the floor. Read the number, and then enter the room on the left. In the pigeon-hole boxes on either side are paper slips with the corresponding number on your bamboo stick. Those on the right-hand wall are printed with your fortunes, while those on the left contain the name of the illness you are said to be suffering from. Get someone at the temple to translate the slips for you or hold on to them until you get back to your hotel, where the desk clerk can translate it.

Also on the altar are pairs of red wooden blocks made from bamboo roots and shaped like twin halves of a mango. These help you make decisions. Pose a question that requires a 'yes' or 'no' answer. Toss the blocks up in the air and watch how they land on the floor. If both land with the same side up or down, the answer is 'no'; if they land, one facing up and one down, the answer is 'yes'. Whichever form of divination you choose, be sure to leave a donation at the altar – it will go towards the upkeep of the shrine.

Other Taoist Temples

Through the compound wall to the left is a more ornate, though more recent Taoist temple, the **Jui Tui Temple**. It is dedicated to Kiu Wong In, a vegetarian god, though from the fierce red and black faces of the gods in attendance, one might think he is a carnivore. Before the altar are cakes, oranges, pineapples and other offerings from devotees. Of particular interest at this temple are the fine carvings of guardians on the huge teak entrance doors. Look also at the photos high on the left-hand wall which show the temple in its various incarnations.

This is the temple where many Vegetarian Festival *(see Calendar of Events)* activities take place in mid-September. In a building on the left are an ornate sedan chair and a chariot on which the image of the main deity is placed before it is pulled through the streets of Phuket.

Leave Put Jaw, turn left and return to Ranong Road. Turn left again to Padiphat Road and right to Krabi Road. Cross the street and walk 50m (160ft) on the left to **Sanjao Sam San**, which is set well back from the road. Built in 1853, this shrine is dedicated to Tien Sang Sung Moo, the Goddess of the Sea, who serves as the patron saint of sailors. When a new boat is launched, a ceremony is held here to bless it. The temple contains some intricate carvings and has a more refined atmosphere than Put Jaw.

Right: joss stick offerings at Jui Tui Temple

Colonial Splendour

Continue your walk down Krabi Road. On the left are huge gardens with beautiful old colonial-style houses built by late 19th-century Chinese rubber and tin barons. At the corner, turn left onto Satun Road. At the next corner, turn right onto Deebuk Road (there's another pretty colonial-style house located on the opposite corner).

As you walk down **Deebuk Road** look out for houses on the right which are in the style called Sino-Portuguese, characterised by their tiled roofs and thick ribbings across the peak and down the roof edges. These were

built by, and are lived in, by old Chinese families. Look closely at the beautiful treatment of the entrances. On the right, at the next corner, are two more superb examples of colonial-style architecture.

Turn left into **Yaowaraj Road**. A short way up on the right in a very cramped garden is perhaps the most beautiful of the colonial houses, a two-storey residence with a yellow bargeboard. Just beyond, on the right, are more Sino-Portuguese shophouses, and at the next traffic light is a colonial home in a pretty garden. An even nicer one is on the left-hand side of the street. One of Phuket's most famous citizens, Governor Rasada Korsimbi, supervised the building of these mansions in the late 19th century. Though visually beautiful, there is a strange mix of styles. Windows and doors are supported by a number of different columns – Corinthian, Doric and Ionic – and facades hint at European neo-classical and renaissance designs.

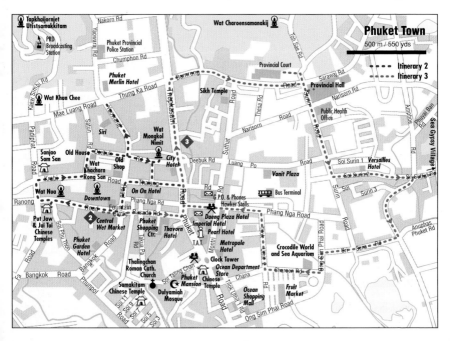

Backtrack down Yaowaraj and turn left onto Deebuk. Halfway down on the left is **Wat Mongkol Nimit**, a Thai Buddhist temple with few distinctive features other than its doors. Cross the street to **Soi Romanni**. The *soi* is badly in need of repair but no street in Phuket can match it for atmosphere. It has the feel of an old Chinese street complete with an old-fashioned barber shop halfway down on the left.

Soi Romanni exits onto Thalang Road. Turn left to see the interesting entrances of more terraced houses. Retrace your steps, passing the entrance to Soi Romanni and continue to the junction with Yaowaraj Road. On the opposite corner is a pretty colonial-style shop. Turn left on Yaowaraj, walk to the traffic circle, turn right, and within a few steps you arrive back at the market. Buy a garland of fragrant *puang malai* – which the Thais hang for good luck in their homes – as a reminder of your first day in Phuket.

Hill-top Lunch and an Aquarium

From here, you can head up Rang Hill for lunch at **Tung-ka Café** (tel: 0 7621 1500). Also at the top of the hill is a statue to the memory of Rasada Korsimbi Narong, the famous governor of Phuket between 1890 and 1909. After lunch, there are several options: either return to the beach for the afternoon, or if you still feel energetic, visit Phuket Town's aquarium located south of the town. Alternatively, visit a sea gypsy village nearby *(Itinerary 3)*. There is a local public bus from Ranong Road which makes frequent trips to the Phuket Aquarium; it bears a sign in English. If you are in a hurry, hire a *tuk-tuk* to travel the 10km (6 miles) to Laem Phanwa.

The **Phuket Aquarium** (daily 8.30am–4pm; admission charge; tel: 0 7639 1128) is part of the Marine Biological Research Centre. Many of the tanks have been fashioned as reproductions of the sea bottom, complete with wharf piles, old tyres and harbour debris. Several hundred tropical fish and marine animal species swim contentedly in the tanks. Most varieties are found in the waters off Phuket, so this visit can serve as an excellent crash course in marine biology if you are planning to dive or snorkel later. Return to the market and head back to your hotel when you are ready.

Left top: a European-style mansion
Above: venomous lion fish on display at the Phuket Aquarium

3. SEA GYPSY VILLAGE *(see map, p28)*

A stop at one of the locations used for the seminal 1980s film, *The Killing Fields*, and on to the quaint sea gypsy village at Ko Sirey. Return to Phuket Town to see some charming colonial-style buildings and some hungry crocodiles.

It's a bit too far to consider walking this itinerary, so hire a tuk-tuk for 2–3 hours. This tour can be done as an extension of the walking tour outlined in Itinerary 2.

Begin your trip in Phuket Town by travelling down Thepkasatri Road (H402) to the junction with Thung Ka Road and Damrong Road. Continue until Damrong Road intersects with Surin Road, where you turn left. Several metres into Surin Road is a left turn into the driveway of the **Phuket Provincial Court**. This beautiful old Portuguese-style building, built in 1916 – an exquisite relic of Phuket's colourful past – is still in use today. On the ground floor, peep into the antiquated courtroom, with its wooden judge's bench, unchanged since the last century.

Return to Surin Street. On the opposite corner, on a large expanse of lawn, is the **Provincial Hall**, home to several provincial offices. The elegant, 80-year-old building with its 99 doors and a history nearly as old as Phuket, served as a replica for the French Embassy in Phnom Penh, Cambodia, in the film, *The Killing Fields*.

Continue south down Surin Road, turning left on Soi Surin 2, which has no English sign, and look for a modern building with grey pillars. After the junction with Amphoe Road, Soi Surin 2 becomes Sri Suthat Road (streets in Thailand have a disconcerting habit of changing their names midway). Cross the causeway over a slough filled with fishing trawlers and enter the sea gypsy village of **Ko Sirey**.

Above: Ko Sirey's sea gypsy community lives a hard life

Phuket's Sea Gypsies

Drive about 1km (½ mile) past mangrove trees to a T-junction opposite a wooden house built on concrete stilts. Turn right and continue another 1km (½ mile) to a fork in the road marked by a blue government sign. Turn right, following the surfaced road for about 1km until you reach Ko Sirey's main sea gypsy (Chao Lay) village. Park and walk through the village. You will meet fishermen repairing lobster traps or cleaning their nets. They are generally shy but friendly. These Chao Lay people belong to the Urak Lawoi group and this village is the largest settlement of its kind in Thailand. The minority Urak Lawoi are generally found between Burma's Mergui Archipelago in the north and the Tarutao-Langkawi Archipelago in the south.

The villagers have seen decades of incursions by other Phuket residents. Today, they continually put up with eviction notices by developers and intrusions by tourists, which is why I hesitate to recommend this tour. Use your own judgment about where you wander in the village, tempering it with consideration for the villagers' mood.

A World of Crocodiles

Return to the fork and turn right, following the surfaced road in a large left-wheeling circuit. Ko Sirey is very pretty and a ride around its perimeter offers a picturesque scene of small villages, views of nearby islands and activities in the bay. The road loops around to the left, bringing you back to the wooden house T-junction. Turn right, cross the causeway and retrace your route to Soi Sri Sena, the southern extension of Amphoe Road. Turn right, and continue until you reach the junction with Ong Sim Phai Road. Turn right and then after 100m (328ft) take the next right onto Chana Charoen Road.

A short way down on the right is Phuket's very own **Crocodile World and Sea Aquarium** (daily 9am–6pm; admission charge). It is the largest crocodile farm in southern Thailand while the aquarium contains many beautiful tropical fish found in the waters surrounding the island.

Thailand is home to two species of crocodile, the Siamese and the Saltwater, both of which have been bred for their skins since the 1950s. During the 1960s, the two species were cross-bred, resulting in a hybrid that tolerated captivity better than its parents and produced leather of a far higher quality than either of them.

After leaving Crocodile World turn right and continue down Chana Charoen Road until you meet Tilok Uthit 2 Road; turn right again and head towards Phang-Nga Road, where you turn left to reach the centre of Phuket Town. At the junction with Phuket Road, where the tour ends, is the beautiful colonial-style **Standard Chartered Bank Building** with its distinctive clock tower.

Right: Chao Lay, or sea gypsy, boy

4. NORTHEAST PASSAGE *(see map, p38–39)*

A drive around the central and northeastern sector. See Phuket's past on display at the Thalang National Museum, its oldest temple, Wat Phra Nang Sang and a rubber plantation. Later, continue to the Wat Phra Thong, a jungle park with gibbons and Bang Bae Waterfall.

From town take the Thepkasatri Road (H402, the airport road) 12km (7½ miles) north to the Heroines' Monument. Turn right into H4027 to find the museum. This is a full-day trip. Take your swimsuit and a towel for the waterfall jaunt.

The **Thalang National Museum** (daily 8.30am–4pm; admission charge; tel: 0 7631 1426) is located some 200m (220yds) down H4027 on the right. The museum exhibits a remarkable collection of artefacts relating to the history of Phuket and the surrounding provinces of Phang Nga and Krabi.

The ethnic diversity of Phuket as a maritime crossroads is apparent in the exhibits on the Moken, Moklen and Urak Lawoi sea gypsies. Stone implements and bones of prehistoric cave dwellers have also been assembled. Displays similarly reconstruct the 11-month Burmese invasion in 1785, when the invaders were finally repelled in a war by the people of Phuket, led by the sisters Mook and Chan. Perhaps the most important item on display is a large 9th-century statue from Takua Pa (north of Phuket) of the Hindu god Vishnu. There are also some very interesting displays relating to life during Phuket's great tin mining boom of the 19th century.

Wat Phra Nang Sang

When you're ready, return to H402 and drive north towards Thalang. On the left, about 50m (160ft) before Thalang's main junction, is **Wat Phra Nang Sang**. The 200-year-old *wat*, the oldest on the island, was built when Thalang was still Phuket's capital. Its two main buildings show the contrast between old and new architectural styles. The *bot* (ordination hall) on the right was built in honour of a woman who, according to folklore, bled white-coloured blood when cut. The metal heads in front of the central Buddha and two attendant images are in the *Dvaravati* style (6th–11th century). The monks of this *wat* claim that these are the oldest metal images in Thailand, but historians say that they could be copies done by a later artist. Unusually, there is a second Reclining Buddha image behind the central image.

The *bot* does not have any doors in its back wall, meaning that the temple, reputedly, will not admit malevolent spirits, and serves as a site for white magic rites. One can have weapons blessed here and receive the incantations and charms which will make one invulnerable to penetration by knives or bullets.

Above: *bot*, or ordination hall, at Wat Phra Nang Sang
Right: rubber trees scored so that they will drip latex, which is later manufactured into rubber

The temple claims to have the longest *Lai Tong* (a religious manuscript folded like an accordion) in Thailand. Legend says the *Lai Tong* contains maps of buried treasure which the Burmese sought when they invaded. The Burmese failed, the monks say, because the holy manuscripts were protected by a demon. They believe that the same demon protects them today.

Leave the *bot* and walk past the tall *chedi* (monument) to the new *bot*, an airy and somewhat overstated building. Notice the murals on the *bot*. The outer front wall depicts Buddha descending from heaven after instructing his dead mother in the Buddhist scriptures. Murals on the interior walls tell the history of Phuket and the fall of Ayutthaya in 1767. These, and the renderings of hell on the exterior back wall, have been captioned in English. Also interesting are the *dvarapala* (guardians) carved on the front doors.

Rubber Tappers

Drive out of the temple and turn left. Proceed to the traffic lights and turn right. You have before you a 4-km (2½-mile) drive down a lovely narrow road cutting through a forest of rubber trees. Rubber is one of Phuket's major industries and there are rubber plantations all over the island. Rubber tappers go to work early, often starting as early as 2am and continuing until sunrise. If you are up early enough you can spot the tappers by the 'fireflies' darting through the trees – the light coming from the calcium carbide or battery-operated lamps the tappers wear on their foreheads. Watch them as they use thin blades to score diagonal lines around the trees so that the latex will bleed and drip into the ceramic cups. The mosquitoes are active at this time of day, so splash on repellent copiously.

If you want to see and learn more, follow the tappers home. There, they pour latex into pans to harden. Once the latex turns solid, the sheets are turned through one mangle to stretch them and then another which scores them with deep lines to squeeze out the liquid and make them pliable. For all their hard work, the tappers receive about 40 baht per kg (2.2lb) for the rubber sheets.

A National Park

At the end of this row of rubber trees is a Forestry Department checkpoint. Turn right into **Khao Phra Thaeo Royal Wildlife & Forest Reserve** (daily 6am–6pm; admission charge). If you are fit, walk 5km (3 miles) down a dirt road through primary jungle to the town of Pa Khlok on Phuket's east coast; otherwise just walk a small section of the trail – the forest scenery, scents and sounds are beautiful.

The park still has a population of gibbons, langurs, macaques, loris, squirrels, wild boar, mouse deer and over 100 species of birds. Whilst walking in the park, do be wary of leeches; it's not a good idea to wear sandals. Leeches can be extremely tenacious and once attached to your skin are difficult to remove without the loss of a great deal of blood. If bitten, apply heat by holding a lighted match or the end of a burning cigarette to the leech. This will cause it to drop off. To stop the bleeding and counteract

the anti-coagulant excreted by leeches, apply a piece of newspaper to the wound. Strange as it sounds, this seems to work.

The park is also home to *Kerriodoxa elegans,* a 5–7 m (16–23ft) tall palm which has only been found here and at Khao Sok National Park *(Excursion 6)* 300km (186 miles) away in Surat Thani. Locals call it *palm khao* (white palm) due to the cloudy white colour on the back of each leaf.

Nature tour companies such as **Siam Safari** (tel: 0 7628 0116) and **Adventure Safaris** (tel: 0 7634 0800) organise short, guided hikes through the park. The park officers at the Visitors' Centre provide a similar service for free.

Return to the checkpoint and turn right, leaving your vehicle in the parking lot. Walk the 250-m (820-ft) trail to **Ton Sai Waterfall**, taking the middle path to the top. In the dry season, the waterfall is just a trickle, becoming a torrent during the rainy season.

If hunger pangs begin to gnaw, the open-sided restaurant on the hill overlooking the pond has delicious yet inexpensive Thai food. Upon returning to the parking lot, drive back towards Thalang. On reaching Thalang, turn right onto H402. Drive north for about 1km (½ mile) to see one of the strangest Buddha images in Thailand. On the right you will notice a sign for Wat Phra Thong. About 500m (1,600ft) down the side road is the temple itself.

Top: Khao Phra Thaeo National Park. **Left:** mushrooms growing from the forest floor
Right: Wat Phra Thong has a curious half-buried statue of the Buddha

The Temple of Wat Phra Thong

Wat Phra Thong or 'Temple of the Golden Buddha Image' is the second most important Buddhist temple on the island after Wat Chalong *(Itinerary 8)*. The temple's fame lies in a legend surrounding its strange Buddha image. The tale has it that a boy tethered a water buffalo to a metal shaft sticking out of the ground. Shortly thereafter, the boy fell ill and died. His distraught father had a dream that told him the metal spike would explain the cause of his son's death. When the father awoke, he began digging around the shaft and found it to be the finial on the head of a huge gold Buddha image. As the soil was very hard, he was only able to dig out the upper half of the image, and so decided to build a *bot* around the part of the Buddha he had managed to excavate.

Over the years, due to stories circulating that the Buddha image was cast from solid gold, many people, including an invading Burmese army, have tried to dig it out of the ground. To date, none has succeeded in unearthing the statue, and most have met grisly deaths as a result of a curse associated with the statue. The statue is in fact made of brick, cement and plaster, with a thin layer of gold leaf covering it.

The image is still left there half buried in the middle of the *bot*. Standing 2m (7ft) tall, it is exposed from the middle of the chest up. It appears to be in a seated position suggesting that its full height would be about 4m (13ft). Though it is not the most aesthetically pleasing of images (it is covered with flecks of gold leaf), the incense smoke in the room does evoke an ethereal atmosphere.

Other Buddha images line the walls of the *bot*. The most interesting is the skeletal Buddha statue on the right. According to lore, Buddha fasted many days and failed to attain nirvana. When he was dangerously weak, a monkey offered honey while an elephant presented him with a section of a bamboo filled with water to enable him to quit his fast gently.

The photos on the back and front walls are of deceased members of the congregation whose ashes lie behind the plaques. At the entrance, buy a

island itineraries

ceramic roof tile. You can get your name written on the back of the tile so that when the new roof is built, your tile will be among the rest.

Continue up H402 to the town of Muang Mai. Turn right on H4027 to Phara. At KM10.2, turn left to **Ao Po**. It is a short but pleasant drive to the sea where you can stop for a refreshing drink at a seaside coffee shop that is likely to be packed with local characters.

Ao Po is the departure point for a visit to the **Naga Pearl Farm** (daily 9am–3.30pm; admission charge; tel: 0 7742 3272) on **Ko Nakha Noi**, which produces the cultured South Sea pearls that Phuket is famous for. If you have not made other arrangements to visit the farm (*Itinerary 5*), there are several long-tailed boat operators here who can arrange a boat ride. Barter a price, using 300 baht per person as a guideline for a return trip.

Rehabilitating Gibbons

Return to H4027 and turn left. At KM8.4, turn right to **Bang Bae Waterfall**, which is 1km (½ mile) down a dirt track. The plunge pools are deepest from June to December, during and just after the rainy season. Beside the car park is the **Gibbon Rehabilitation Project** (daily 9am–4pm; free; tel: 0 7626 0492), which looks after gibbons and gradually reintroduces them to the wild. Not long ago, many of them used to be chained to seedy bars in Patong.

Return to H4027, turn right to the Heroines' Monument, then left to Phuket Town on H402. About 300m (330yds) beyond the Heroines' Monument, on the east side of the road, a small sign directs those curious about the history of Phuket, to what remains of the old settlement of Tha Rua, after its destruction by the Burmese in 1876.

Here, during the late 18th century, European adventurers and merchants had maintained a small town giving access to the old harbour at Sapam Bay. The most illustrious of these early settlers was Sir Francis Light, who went on to found the British settlement at Penang in nearby Malaysia.

Above: gibbon play
Right: the pier at Ao Po

5. NAGA PEARL FARM *(see map, p38–39)*

A visit to a pearl farm on Ko Nakha Noi – off the remote northeastern coast of Phuket – reputed to have cultured the world's largest pearl.

Visitors without their own means of transport should book a guided tour by either calling 076-219 870 or visiting the Naga Pearl Farm office at S T Hotel, Sakdidet Road. Alternatively, book the tour through a travel agent. The price for this half-day tour includes admission fee, lunch and hotel transfer.

In the waters off Phuket's eastern coast are numerous pearl farms. Most grow 'half pearls', but **Naga Pearl Farm** (daily 9am–3.30pm; admission charge; tel: 0 7742 3272) on **Ko Nakha Noi** grows the full-sized South Sea pearls, fine examples of which are worth thousands of dollars.

Although the true facts are lost in the mists of time, it is generally agreed that the Chinese learned the art of growing cultured pearls more than eight centuries ago – perhaps even longer. The preferred oysters for cultured pearls belong to the genus Pinctada – while some are reared on the pearl farms, others are collected by local divers and sold to pearling companies like that on Ko Nakha Noi.

In nature, a minute grain of sand or some other irritant may find its way into the shell of an oyster, causing the mollusc to react by building a smooth nacreous veneer over the intruder, layer by layer, until a pearl is formed. In the cultured pearling process, this small irritant is introduced deliberately, and the oyster kept and cared for while the pearl is growing. Experts agree that the oyster lays down a very fine layer of nacre several times a week, though the process is slow and as many as a thousand layers must be laid down before the pearl is ready for harvesting.

World's Largest Pearl

Ko Nakha Noi is an attractive island, with a good restaurant and a clean beach. The tour begins at 9am with a hotel pick-up and a boat ride to the island. After lunch, you are shown how foreign substances (usually a small stone or bead) are implanted into oysters to trigger the pearl creation process. The farm has a replica of the world's largest pearl which it reportedly created in 1987; the original is now housed at the famous Mikimoto Pearl Museum in Japan.

You are then shown the growing frames where the oysters are nurtured. Finally, experts demonstrate how the finished pearl is removed from its shell, graded and marketed for export. The tour ends at 2.30pm and you return to town with a shopping stop at a Thai handicraft showroom, arriving at your hotel around 5pm. Alternatively, accommodation is available at the 10-room Nakha Pearl Farm Bungalows (tel: 0 7621 4583), should you wish to stay overnight on Nakha Noi.

Right: worker at the Pearl Farm implanting a seed into an oyster

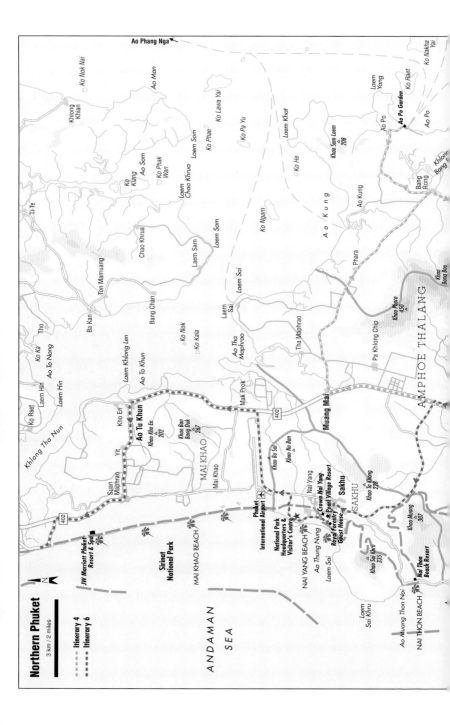

Northern Phuket

3 km / 2 miles

········· Itinerary 4
▪▪▪▪▪ Itinerary 6

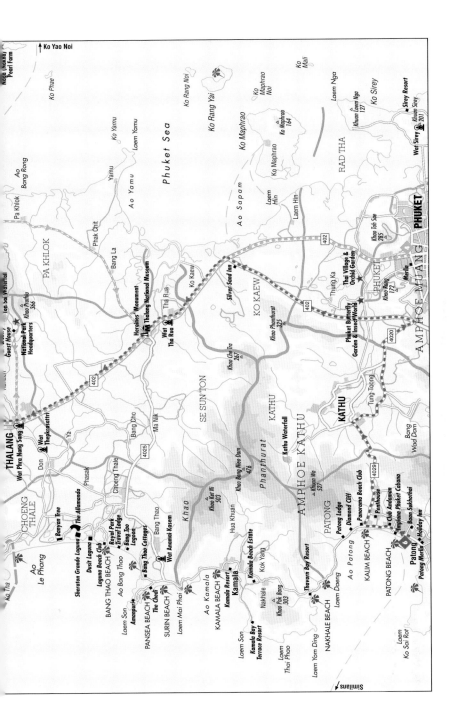

6. NORTH PHUKET *(see map, p38–39)*

A drive to Phuket's remote northern tip takes you through the quaint little village of Ban Sakhu and on to Sirinat National Park's beautiful casuarina forest and the pristine Nai Yang and Mai Khao beaches.

Drive north from Patong, on Thepkasatri Road (H402) and turn left onto H4031. A short way in, you enter a beautiful 1-km (½-mile) stretch of rubber trees that arch over the narrow road, providing an excellent photo opportunity. On leaving the highway you will pass by picturesque rice paddies filled with lolling water buffaloes. A half-day tour.

About 4km (2½ miles) into the highway you will pass through **Ban Sakhu**, a village full of beautiful flower gardens and fruit trees. Many of the flowers on show are not native to Southeast Asia, including allamanda, bougainvillea, heliconia and the impressive flame trees. Look out for the red chillies laid out by villagers to dry in the sun. Once dry, they are crushed and ground and then used in cooking Thai dishes. Some 2km (1¼ miles) past Sakhu is a sign on the left marking the entrance to the **Pearl Village Resort** on **Nai Yang Beach**. On reaching the entrance, motorcyclists will find a narrow dirt path to the right that bypasses the hotel and takes you on to **Sirinat National Park**. If you drive a jeep, carry on up H4031 to KM1.2, turning left at a blue sign that points down a dirt road leading to the park.

Above: wallowing water buffaloes
Right: the scenic road to Nai Yang Beach

Sirinat National Park covers the area formerly occupied by the Nai Yang National Park and the mangrove reserve at Mai Khao. It includes some 22 sq km (8 sq miles) of coastline, from Nai Yang to Mai Khao *(see below)* further north as well as 68 sq km (26 sq miles) of sea. An extensive coral reef close to the shore at Nai Yang Beach is a popular site with divers and snorkellers. Other than the Pearl Village and Nai Yang Beach Resort at Nai Yang's southern end, the area is closed to developers.

Sea Turtle Sanctuary

Between November and February each year, Olive Ridley Sea Turtles, weighing about 35kg (77lbs) clamber onto Nai Yang's sandy shore at night. They dig deep holes with their flippers and then lay in them up to 120 leathery-shelled eggs, an instinctual behaviour said to be 90 million years old. Bring a flashlight along if you want to witness this wonder of nature, but try not to disturb the turtles labouring at their task. Another occasional visitor is the Giant Leatherback Turtle, which on average weighs 540kg (1,200lbs), but can weigh nearly twice that, and lays as many as 150 eggs at a time.

Near the northern end of the forest of tall casuarina trees at Nai Yang is the **Sirinat National Park Visitors' Centre**, with displays of corals, shells, butterflies, turtles, and other interesting fauna found on the island.

When you have seen enough, leave by the northern end and continue left along H4031 to the airport. Pass it and drive 3½km (2 miles) to re-join H402. Turn left and drive north. After 12km (7½ miles), turn left at the National Park sign and drive 2km (1 mile) past beach restaurants on remote **Mai Khao Beach**. Like Nai Yang, Mai Khao is also an important nesting site for Olive Ridley Sea Turtles. Explore the mangroves at its northernmost end, close to where a park office is located, using the excellent elevated wooden walkways, or return to the restaurant area to lunch on seafood or swim. Only one hotel, the plush J W Marriott Resort & Spa is found at Mai Khao.

7. THAI VILLAGE AND BUTTERFLY GARDEN
(see map, p38–39)

A quick introduction to Thai culture and an elephant show, followed by a visit to the Phuket Butterfly Garden and Insect World.

To reach the Thai Village, drive north on Thepkasatri Road (H402). Turn left at KM2.5, just before a huge BMW sign; drive 1km (½ mile) more and park. Alternatively, many tour companies in Phuket offer the Thai Village show with round-trip hotel transfer. Plan for a 2–3 hour outing.

The **Thai Village** (two shows daily, 11am and 5.30pm; tel: 0 7621 4869; admission charge), like its counterparts in Bangkok and Chiang Mai, provides visitors with a brief sampling of southern culture.

The 45-minute programme presents samples of authentic southern Thai culture, as well as dances from other regions of the country. It is presented

Right: *Nora* dancers strike a pose at the Thai Village

in an airy, covered arena on a stage decorated to resemble a typical southern Thailand thatch-and-bamboo house. Included in the programme are a *Nang Thalung,* shadow puppet play, found only in the south of Thailand and an interesting performance of *Manohra* (or *Nora*), a southern classical dance once performed only by men, but now danced by women who wear beautiful beaded bird costumes and long fake fingernails.

Next is a *Chak Phra* religious procession and a Thai boxing match. A silk weaving dance from northern Thailand is followed by a drum dance from central Thailand. Then comes a stick fight, where a giant of a man, wielding a stick, is pitted against a monkey armed only with twin blocks of wood. A Thai wedding ceremony is followed by a northeastern harvest dance, which originates from the early kingdom of Srivijaya. The grand finale is a medley of dances including a rubber-tapping dance, fishing dance and tin miners' dance. It is a thoroughly professional and enjoyable performance.

After the show, leave the hall to an outdoor arena where elephants demonstrate how they handle huge teak logs. In an open-air setting, artisans demonstrate how southern crafts are made.

Butterflies and Fishes

On leaving the Thai Village, turn right and follow the signs along Panaeng Lane to the **Phuket Butterfly Garden and Insect World**, 76/1 Sankong, Phuket Town (daily 9am–6pm; admission charge; tel: 0 7621 5616). The aquarium is filled with numerous tanks of colourful corals and sometimes strange-looking fish like the dogface puffer and long-horned cowfish. Bigger specimens include giant morays and sleek black-tip sharks.

The garden contains thousands of colourful butterflies in various stages of their life cycles. The atmosphere is kept artificially moist by a humidifier. In the same garden there is a scorpion pit, an insect display – including giant stag beetles – and a pond full of colorful *koi* or Chinese carp.

8. SOUTH TO WAT CHALONG AND RAWAI
(see map, p44)

A morning swim at Kathu Waterfall followed by a visit to Wat Chalong, the island's most important Buddhist temple. Have a seaside snack at Chalong Bay as the boats come in, then on to Rawai Beach.

For a glimpse of festive colour, try to arrange this tour on a Buddhist holy day, but any morning will do. Inquire at your hotel and plan your visit accordingly. Half a day is enough for this tour. Take your swimsuit and towel.

Drive on H4029 out of Patong. At the first junction, turn left onto the road to Kathu. About 1½km (1 mile) later, turn left, driving 2km (1¼ mile) to **Kathu Waterfall**. Leave your jeep or motorcycle in the parking lot, cross the

bridge and climb 250m (820ft) up the steps to the lower falls. On the right of the *sala* (pavilion) is a changing room where you can don your swimsuit.

When you're ready, cross the pond wall and climb 100m (330ft) up the steps that are cut into the hillside. At the top are more beautiful pools. Relax and let the waterfall wash over you. The falls, which are at their best when the water levels are high in the monsoon season, become only a trickle in the hotter months of March and April. The **Jee Lee-an** restaurant (tel: 0 7632 1684; daily 10am–10pm), near the bridge at the foot of the steps, serves simple but delicious Thai food.

Return to H4029, turn left and continue to the town of **Kathu**. Kathu was the first of three towns to have served as the capital city of the island. Lining its narrow street are very picturesque old buildings, some still roofed with thatch. Phuket's famous Vegetarian Festival *(see Calendar of Events)* is said to have originated in Kathu and to this day the town still celebrates it annually with events and processions similar to those in Phuket Town.

An Ornate Temple
After 1km (½ mile), the road rejoins H4020, the main road into Phuket Town. When you reach the junction with the bypass road, H4021, turn right. After another 3km (2 miles), turn left at the junction and proceed 1km (½ mile) to the main H4021 between Phuket Town and Rawai. Turn right and head for **Wat Chalong**, Phuket's most important Buddhist temple.

The temple sits on the left of the bypass road (H4021), 3km (2 miles) before the Chalong Junction. Although Wat Chalong is not known for its artistic merit (its architecture is typical of temples found throughout Thailand), it is still the biggest and most ornate of Phuket's 29 Buddhist monasteries. On a bright sunny day, its sparkling facade makes it one of the most photogenic sites on the island.

The temple is associated with three revered monks: renowned herbal doc-

Left: a dazzling butterfly at the Phuket Butterfly Park
Above: Kathu Waterfall is especially scenic in the rainy season

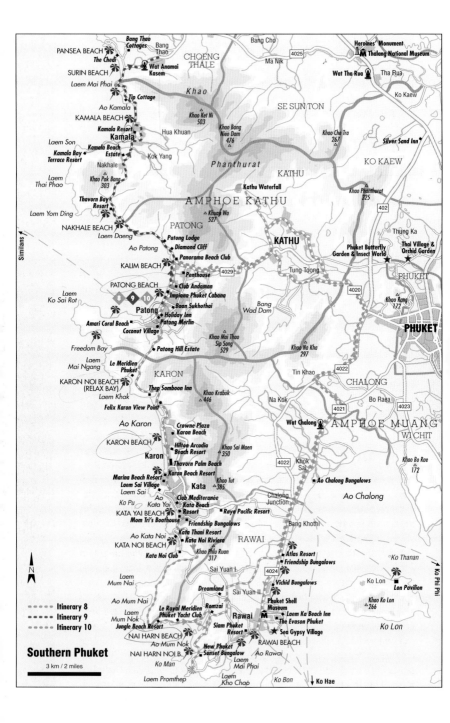

Southern Phuket

3 km / 2 miles

- - - - Itinerary 8
- - - - Itinerary 9
- - - - Itinerary 10

tors and setters of bones. One of them, Luang Pho Chaem, had ample opportunity to demonstrate his skills during the tin miners' rebellion of 1876, when a great many bones were broken. He also mediated in the rebellion, bringing the warring parties together to resolve their dispute. Gilt statues honouring him and the other two monks stand in the *viharn* (prayer hall).

On Buddhist holy days, the monks chant ancient Pali scriptures and then eat food brought to the temple by villagers. The chanting begins about 9am and the monks must dine before noon.

From Wat Chalong continue down H4021 to the Chalong Junction and turn left. The harbour at the end of the road is very busy in the late afternoon with tour boats returning from day trips. For lunch try the **Kan Eang 1** restaurant (tel: 0 7638 1212) at 44/1 Viset Road, Chalong Bay. It sits right on the waterfront and makes a perfect setting to nurse a cold drink and sample spicy *tom yam* soup while watching the boats come in. The restaurant

serves a large selection of seafood dishes. At the harbour, look out for the distinctive Burmese boats bearing tail fins like those found on 1950s Chevrolets and Cadillacs.

Rawai's Attractions

Returning to the Chalong Junction, turn left and head south on H4024 for 4km (2½ miles) to Rawai. Look for the **Phuket Shell Museum** (daily 8.30am–6pm; admission charge; tel: 0 7638 1266) on the right, nearly opposite the entrance to The Evason Phuket hotel. A giant concrete wentletrap shell stands before it.

The museum is, in reality, Rawai's oldest and most comprehensive shell shop. Most of the shell specimens are quite cheap and make lovely gifts, especially for children. The specimens are brought up from great depths in trawler nets. In their raw state, they are covered by thick, rubbery coats which, when removed, reveal breathtakingly intricate designs. The museum exhibits shells from other parts of the world including one giant, weighing in at 250kg (550lbs). There are also shell fossils and the world's largest golden pearl. All exhibits are carefully labelled in English.

Continue down the H4024. Just before the road forks right to **Rawai Beach**, there is a small sea gypsy village on the left fronted by batik, t-shirt, and souvenir stalls. The primitive huts of the village house the Urak Lawoi sea gypsies, whose indigenous language is very similar to Malay. Their children, however, now grow up speaking Thai at local schools, while young sea gypsy men tend to drift away from the sea and take up land-based employment. This is a friendly and safe community, and they don't mind if visitors walk amidst their modest dwellings. Most days you will find the women selling the day's catch on the road in front of the village. Some of the fish appear quite exotic, including beautifully coloured parrotfish.

Above: devotee sticking beaten gold leaves on a Buddha image at Wat Chalong

For a snack, you can eat tasty seafood at any of the pleasantly breezy shacks further south along the coast road at Rawai. Because of local fishing activities, Rawai Beach is not the best place on the island to swim and sunbathe, but it does have its advantages, most notably it is far less crowded than Patong, Karon and Kata. Trips to nearby islands including Ko Hae, Ko Lon and Ko Aeo are possible from Rawai.

9. KHAO PHANTHURAT AND SURIN *(see map, p44)*

Travel north from Patong for spectacular views from the Khao Phanthurat pass and then descend to a fishing village at Kamala and the Muslim communities in the Surin area.

With the new and widened road surface, this is a pleasant ride. Drive north out of Patong on the road that follows the northern curve of the bay. Half a day is plenty of time to make the round trip. Dress appropriately if you plan to visit the mosque at Surin.

About 2km (1 mile) beyond Patong is **Laem Daeng Restaurant** on the left. Sitting on a bluff, this unpretentious restaurant enjoys a superb view of Patong Beach. Further up the hill there are more new coastal cliff restaurants with fine sea views. After refreshments, continue up the steep hill to **Khao Phanthurat** pass, which is 303m (990ft) above sea level. When you

reach the top, pause to enjoy the spectacular view of the sea and the fields of Kamala valley. At the bottom of the hill, turn left and a bit farther on, turn right across a concrete bridge to reach the small but interesting fishing village at **Kamala Beach**.

Above: fishing boats at Rawai Beach
Left: Kamala Beach fisherman

Mosques and Muslims

Follow the road out of Kamala Beach, going northwards. On the right are the fields of Kamala, with the **Kamala Mosque** glowing against the distant hill. Beyond the FantaSea Entertainment Park, the road begins to climb, becoming narrower and bending a great deal. If you like the challenge of curving roads, this one will satisfy you. When you are near the top, stop and look back to the lovely cove below.

After passing – or stopping at – beautiful **Laem Sing Beach**, head towards **Surin Beach** with its numerous tasty seafood and northeastern Isaan food snacks sold at its beachside cafes. Try the delicious *kaeng matsaman* (Muslim-style curry) at a Surin restaurant for lunch.

If you continue along the coast following the narrow road, past The Chedi resort, you will find quaint Muslim fishing villages with fishermen repairing boats and nets, and children frolicking. Continuing, you turn inland again on the H4025. On the right is the **Surin Mosque**, the island's biggest mosque. It's fine to enter the mosque, but – as with Buddhist temples – visitors should dress modestly, remove their shoes and avoid wandering around the mosque during prayer times. Phuket's Muslims are an easygoing people who interact well with their Buddhist neighbours. Quite a few trace at least part of their ancestry to nearby Malaysia; and Malay, Arab and Indian influences are readily apparent in some of their cooking.

Now you have a choice: you can retrace your route back along the same road, getting a new perspective on the scenery; or continue on through Surin to the Heroines' Monument where you turn right onto H402, the busy north-south main road. About 4km (2½ miles) down the road, turn right at the big junction to the bypass road, H4021. From here, it is a short ride to the junction with H4020 where a right turn takes you back to Patong.

10. SUNSET VIEWS AT PROMTHEP *(see map, p44)*

A scenic late afternoon drive on the road to Laem Promthep and Nai Harn, ending with a seafood dinner while taking in the sunset.

Rent a car and start out at about 3pm from Patong, or wherever you may be staying.

Take Thawiwong Road, leaving at the southern end of town, just past the Patong Merlin Hotel. Just past the Simon Cabaret, the road climbs above the sea and then over a rise, revealing Karon ahead. It then skirts Karon Beach and climbs a small hill before dropping into Kata. Continue through Kata, past Club Med. At the junction, turn right, pass the Boathouse Inn and climb the hill. Halfway up is a junction with a road climbing steeply to the left. This new road takes you high along a ridge with a lovely view of the sea on your right. Its curves are gentle, a motorcyclist's dream road that allows you

Right: the view from Laem Promthep

to lean into corners and shift through the gears. The road then drops into Nai Harn valley. At a Y-junction, take the right-hand fork. The road enters the valley at the head of the lagoon. Turn left at the first junction and climb the left-hand side of the valley to the viewpoint that looks down on **Nai Harn Beach**.

Promthep Cape

After you have had your fill of the vistas, continue to **Laem Promthep** with its finger of land pointing into the sea. The name Laem Promthep literally translated means 'Cape Brahma', named in honour of the Hindu God of Creation. It's a splendid headland, stretching southwest into the waters of the Andaman Sea towards Ko Kaeo Yai. From time immemorial, Laem Promthep has been a prominent landmark for vessels approaching Phuket.

Today, though, it is more famous as a viewpoint for visitors who travel to the headland and watch the blood red orb of the setting sun sink slowly in the west. Just by the cape is a modern lighthouse with a raised platform for sightseeing. The view from this vantage point is outstanding. Alternatively, a flight of steps leads to the top of the rocky hill above the cape, offering wonderful views across Nai Harn Beach. Appropriately, near the top of the hill, there is a shrine to Brahma where local people can often be seen making offerings of flowers, fruit and incense.

When the sun has set retrace your route to the head of Nai Harn Beach, this time turning left and travelling along the right-hand edge of the beach. The road seems to end at the Le Royal Meridien Phuket Yacht Club, a luxury hotel that hugs the hillside. Continue on, however, dropping into the hotel's underground parking lot and out to the left. If it is the cool season, the bay will be dotted with numerous yachts.

For a different route back, return along the beach and onto the road that leads out of Nai Harn at a right angle to the beach. At the three-way junction that you encountered when you came off the ridge road from Kata, turn right. The road carries on to H4024. Turn left and within 2km (1¼ mile), is the Chalong Junction. Take the bypass road (H4021) back to Patong. As you cross the mountain, look out for a tiny Taoist shrine on the crest, erected to protect drivers from the angry spirits of the dozens of people who have died in traffic accidents on the road here.

Above: a Phuket sunset
Right: spectacular Nai Harn Beach

Excursions

1. PHANG NGA BAY *(see map, p52)*

An excursion to Ao Phang Nga National Park, a marine reserve comprising unusual limestone monoliths and islands, towering cliffs and the clear azure waters of the Sea of Phuket.

Most Phuket tour companies will pick you up from your hotel at about 8am for the 70–90-minute drive to the bay. From the Phang Nga Bay Resort jetty, you travel by long-tailed boat past islands shaped like beasts. A full-day trip.

The islands in Phang Nga Bay, 75km (46½ miles) northeast of Phuket, are among the wonders of Asia, rivalling and perhaps even surpassing Vietnam's famed Halong Bay. Together the islands make up **Ao Phang Nga National Park**, which covers an area of about 400 sq km (154 sq miles). Sheer-sided limestone monoliths rise 300m (980ft) out of the sea like the ethereal mountains in Chinese paintings. They are particularly breathtaking in the early morning light.

Many cliffs are clad in curtains of limestone; others are shaped like melted candle wax. Soon you arrive at **Ko Ping Kan**, also known as 'James Bond Island', as it was featured in the Bond film, *The Man With the Golden Gun*. Tour guides never tire of telling you this – and with such awe that you would think it was *War and Peace* rather than the celebrated thriller that had its genesis here. The waters in front of Ko Ping Kan hold a geologic oddity called **Ko Tapu** (Nail Island). Rising from a precariously thin base 200m (650ft) out of the water, like the Leaning Tower of Pisa, the island seems destined to tip into the water at some future date.

A Village on Stilts

The boat then moves on to **Ko Panyi**, an island with a Muslim village built entirely on stilts next to a limestone mountain, and housing some 500 families. There's an attractive, green-roofed mosque sheltering in the lee of the great cliff, which dominates the village. Don't hesitate to go in – providing, of course, you are properly clad and that it isn't the time of prayers. As is the case elsewhere along the Andaman coast, Islam is decidedly laid back here. If you're on an organised tour, lunch will be included, but if you're not, there are tiny shops and food stalls selling cold drinks and snacks,

Left: ethereal Phang Nga Bay at dusk
Right: souvenir shop at Ko Ping Kan, 'James Bond Island'

Phuket and Environs

10 km / 6 miles

all perched high on stilts above the gently moving Andaman Sea. It's even possible to stay overnight on the island, but the accommodation available is somewhat basic.

The return boat journey is generally via **Tham Lawt**, a natural tunnel that runs beneath a huge mountain. It then stops at **Khao Khian** for passengers to see drawings of ancient ships on its rock walls, visible only from the water. Many tours also visit **Tham Suwan Kuha**, a limestone cave 12km (7½ miles) from Phang Nga. The caves hold Buddha images illuminated by a shaft of sunlight pouring through a hole in the ceiling. This cave is well worth the trip, so ask if it is included in your tour.

A different way of getting to Phang Nga is to take a leisurely Chinese junk ride on board the *June Bahtra*. This trip, which is operated by **Asia Voyages** (tel: 0 2651 9768; www.asiavoyagesonline.com), takes in Ko Ping Kan, Ko Tapu and Ko Panyi. The day starts at 7.30am when guests are picked up from their hotel for the road trip to Laem Prao pier. Located in northeast Phuket, this pier is where guests board the slow-moving junk for the full-day tour. The fare includes long-tailed boat transfers to Ko Panyi and Ko Ping Kan where only small boats can land, and also a good seafood lunch on board. Guests are returned to the jetty by 6pm for the transfer back to their hotel.

2. SEA KAYAKING IN PHANG NGA *(see map, p52)*

An adventure by kayak through the wondrous sea caves and mysterious lagoons of Phang Nga Bay. Explore tidal lagoons and strange limestone monoliths that rise from the sea.

Several companies based in Phuket offer kayak tours of Phang Nga Bay. **John Gray's Sea Canoe** *(124 Soi 1 Yaowaraj Road, tel: 0 7625 4505, fax: 0 7622 6077, e-mail: info@johngray-seacanoe.com) pioneered the activity in these waters and is highly recommended. Longer trips of up to a week are also available for the more hardy. Note: this tour covers parts of Phang Nga that cannot be accessed by Excursion 1.*

Capable of reaching places that other boats cannot, an inflatable sea kayak is the ideal craft for a close exploration of the extraordinary landscape and seascape of Phang Nga. This eco-friendly trip will probably be one of your most rewarding experiences in Phuket.

Sitting two people to a kayak, the guide will paddle through tiny sea caves and tunnels under huge limestone hills rising from the bay. Many of these monoliths are doughnut-shaped, hollow in the middle and open to the sky. The skilful guide will time the kayak's entry into these monoliths to coincide with the ebbing tides, squeezing through narrow passages only inches from your face.

Right: pristine Phang Nga Bay

Lagoons and Caves

Once inside, you will discover a geographic wonder – tidal lagoons iso-lated from the world and enclosed by sheer rock. Surrounded by mangroves and cliff-clinging trees, these silent lagoons are inhabited by an incredible array of plant and animal life, including monkeys, hornbills, kingfishers, owls and monitor lizards.

The day begins with a road trip to Ao Po Harbour in northeast Phuket. Here, you board the support vessel for the 1-hour trip into the heart of Phang Nga, where you explore a number of caves on the inflatable kayaks with a guide. After lunch, you get to paddle the kayak on your own, if you wish, to a semi-open rock island. Later in the afternoon, the support vessel takes you to a sandy beach for swimming and relaxing.

The trips, organised by **John Gray's Sea Canoe**, are limited to a maxi-mum of 12 participants each, accompanied by guides, both for practical reasons and to limit the impact on the environment.

3. PHI PHI ISLANDS *(see maps, p52 and 56)*

A boat trip to the twin island jewels of Ko Phi Phi, located in the Phuket Sea between Phuket and mainland Krabi.

Ko Phi Phi can be reached in about 2 hours from Ao Makham in southeast Phuket. Songserm Travel (tel: 0 7622 2570) has a day-trip which takes you to Phi Phi Don for lunch, then on to explore the caves of Phi Phi Leh and for some snorkelling. It then returns to Tong Sai Beach on Phi Phi Don for rest and relaxation before making the boat journey back to Phuket. If you choose to spend the night (or longer) in Phi Phi Don, inform the agency so that you can be picked up the next day at 3pm from in front of the Phi Phi Island Cabana at Ton Sai. You can also book a return boat trip to Phi Phi without tours from Songserm or any of the Phuket tour agencies which sell this tour.

Above: Phang Nga's geological wonders

Phi Phi Leh and **Phi Phi Don**, the twin islands collectively known as Ko Phi Phi (pronounced 'Pee Pee') are two of the most stunning islands in Asia. Perched at the southern end of the Phang Nga chain, 34km (20 miles) southeast of Phuket – and part of **Hat Noppharat Thara Ko Phi Phi National Marine Park** – the beauty of these limestone monoliths rivals another island with a double-barrelled name, French Polynesia's Bora Bora.

The larger of the two, **Phi Phi Don**, is 20km (12½ miles) in circumference. Two enormous mountains – one 498m (1,630ft) tall – are linked by a strip of sand to create, what, from the air, would look like a giant high-backed chair. The strand is so narrow that you could stand on one shore and almost heave a rock to the opposite shore. Nine coves of powdery sand, adjoining coral reefs, and warm aquamarine waters give the island its reputation for supreme beauty. Its small population lives in a scattering of fishing villages that are rapidly being nudged further into the jungle by the burgeoning resort development.

It is on Phi Phi Don that most tourist activity is centered. Although much of the infrastructure on the principal **Ton Sai Beach** was destroyed by the tsunami, the majority of tourist accommodation, travel agencies, restaurants and shops are being renovated and many are already partially – if not completely – rebuilt and ready to accommodate guests.

The southern coves of Phi Phi Don are separated by rocky headlands. Each has cheap bungalows priced from 200 baht a night and up and are clearly intended for budget travellers. If you like your accommodation rustic, these will suit you perfectly. If you prefer comfort, hot water and air-

conditioning, stick to the resorts on Ton Sai beach.

The most popular of the southern beaches is **Long Beach**, or Hat Yao, where the best snorkelling reefs are found. Boats leave regularly from Ton Sai dock. Otherwise, do it the scenic way at low tide: walk for half-an-hour along the shore. If you look carefully at the boulders dividing the beaches, you will see that each is essentially a single rock plate which has been cracked and broken.

Above: Ton Sai Beach
Left: the twin bays of Phi Phi Don

Spectacular Vistas

My main reason for visiting Phi Phi Don is the grand vista of island and sea that you get from a large flat rock located high on a bluff at the southern end of **Loh Dalam Bay**. To get there, walk along Loh Dalam Bay past Phi Phi Princess and Pavilion beach resorts. Follow the signs up the hill past Phi Phi Viewpoint Resort to the vantage point. At the top, slump down on the rock, breathe deeply and drink in one of the most beautiful panoramas imaginable. Beyond the jungle canopy are the twin bays of Phi Phi Don, separated from each other by a thin band of land with the mountain behind serving as a backdrop.

If you didn't come on the Songserm boat (which already includes the following sidetrip), and are staying at Phi Phi Don, book yourself on a long-tailed boat trip to **Phi Phi Leh**, easily one of the most rewarding trips you can do on these islands. Smaller Phi Phi Leh lies some 4km (2¼ miles) south of Phi Phi Don. It has fewer beaches than Phi Phi Don but attracts thousands of swifts, which build nests prized by Chinese gourmets for birds' nest soup. Swarms of swifts descend on Phi

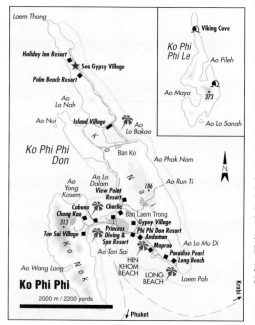

Above: a cave nesting site for swallows on Phi Phi Leh

Phi Leh between January and April to spend about two weeks in the caves building nests held together by their saliva.

Each long-tailed boat on such trips can take about 6–8 passengers. The first stop is the rather inappropriately-named **Viking Cave**, which has walls embellished with a mixture of prehistoric murals representing both human and animal forms, together with much more recent, probably 19th-century, representations of Chinese sea-going junks. This is followed by a trip into **Pi Leh Bay** and **Maya Bay** for a spot of snorkelling. Maya Bay has been hailed one of the most beautiful bays in the world and recently played host – amid much outcry from environmental activists about the damage to the bay – to the filming of *The Beach*, which starred Leonardo Di Caprio.

The boat then takes a clockwise route, passing the sheer cliffs of both Phi Phi islands to stop at nearby **Ko Mai Phai** (Bamboo Island) for a simple lunch, after which there is time for swimming or lazing on the powdery white sands. The boat then proceeds to coral beds teeming with colourful fish just off Ko Mai Phai for more snorkelling. On the way back the boat passes **Hin Phae** (Goat Reef) at the tip of Long Beach. The boat arrives back at Ton Sai around 4.30pm. All the travel agents on Phi Phi Don sell this package, which includes snorkelling equipment and packed lunch. For divers, the deeper waters of **Ko Bida** and **Hin Muang** can also be explored.

4. THE SIMILAN ISLANDS *(see map, p52)*

Scuba dive in one of the world's most beautiful diving spots. Non-divers can opt for a snorkelling day-trip that lets you enjoy the wonders of the Similan Islands from the surface of the water.

*Boats only service the Similan Islands between November and April. For the remainder of the year the seas are too rough. **Songserm Travel** (tel: 0 7622 2570) organises a day-trip which leaves Patong at 8am and returns at 7pm on Tuesday, Thursday and Saturday. The journey from Phuket to the main island takes 3½–4 hours, which gives you roughly 3 hours on the island for lunch, snorkelling and some relaxation. Scuba divers can go on multi-day dive safaris on yachts that offer 'live aboard' dive operations. Best diving is between December and May when the weather is fine and underwater visibility is at its best.*

The remote **Similan Islands** – for many years a well-kept secret among scuba divers – are among the most beautiful coral reef islands found anywhere in Asia. *Similan* means 'nine islands' in Malay and while each island has a name, most people would rather refer to them by their numbers. The islands are located

Right: the underwater life in the Similan Islands is unparalleled

some 95km (105 miles) northwest of Phuket or 65km (70 miles), 2½ hours from the nearest mainland town of Thap Lamu in Phang Nga Province, from where most boat journeys originate.

The islands' western shores are dominated mainly by giant boulders perched on fine sand beaches. Most divers head for the eastern coast of No 4 island, or **Ko Miang**, where the coral reefs extend far offshore and harbour a wide and beautiful variety of marine life. Because the islands lie so far from civilisation, they are still pristine, providing ample rewards for those willing to endure long boat trips to experience them. While one can snorkel among the reefs, the islands are better suited to scuba divers because the surrounding waters are very deep.

Roughing it

If you decide to stay on the islands, be prepared to rough it. On Ko Miang, the **Similan Islands National Marine Park** rents out a bungalow holding 20 people as well as 40 two-man tents. Toilet facilities are rudimentary – only the squat type is available. You can reserve accommodation by writing to the National Parks Division, Lodging Service, Bang Khen, Bangkok 10900 or by calling 0 2579 0529 or 0 2279 5269; www.dnp.go.th. Alternatively call the Thap Lamu office at 0 7659 5045. You may be able to make arrangements for accommodation on arrival at the island, but during the high season this could be a risky option. You are advised to bring along your own food for this trip as the fare at the one restaurant at Ko Miang is very expensive.

The other option, and the more comfortable one, is to book yourself a place on a 'live aboard' dive operation. Several dive shops like Fantasea Divers and Santana Dive Centre in Patong offer week-long dive safaris on board comfortable yachts to the Similan Islands (see *Outdoor Activities* chapter for more details on these).

Divers can expect to see spectacular Gorgonian Fan corals, 140-kg (309-lb) garoupas, lionfish with poisonous fin rays, stonefish with very poisonous dorsal and pectoral fins, and sharks, including the nurse, whitetip, blacktip, gray reef, leopard, whale, hammerhead and bull species. There are also colourful butterfly and parrotfish, sea cucumbers and sea urchins.

For non-scuba divers, the best way to see the Similan Islands is to take the Songserm Travel day trip. There are no tours in the monsoon season as the waves are too high. Independent boat trips cost too much money and are difficult to organise on your own.

5. KRABI AND ENVIRONS *(see maps, p52 and 60)*

Located on the mainland to the east of Phuket, Krabi Province comprises more than 5,000 sq km (1,930 sq miles) of rainforested hills, a gorgeous Andaman Sea coastline, pristine beaches and around 200 islands.

From Phuket, mainland Krabi is accessible by both road, sea and air (see below). Allow three days or more for this excursion.

Krabi is really an alternative holiday base to Phuket, and has sufficient attractions to keep you occupied for at least one week. Though communications have improved, it still takes time to travel the 180km (112 miles) by road from Phuket, which is really part of its charm. Tourism is still relatively undeveloped in the province, so the pace is slower and people tend to be friendlier.

Getting There

Krabi-bound air-conditioned buses leave the Phuket public bus station throughout the day for the 3-hour ride. If you'd rather travel by taxi, rent one from the Phuket airport; it is more comfortable and quicker as well. Resorts in Krabi will organise transport if you've made prior arrangements with them. Towering limestone hills, lush rice paddies and palm oil plantations make it a memorable ride, though you can't see the sea for most of the way.

Alternatively, travel to Krabi by boat. It will take several hours, but the scenery of the inner Andaman Sea is magnificent, and allows you to finesse your suntan along the way. Express boats leave Phuket and travel via Phi Phi Don daily for Krabi. Contact travel agents in Phuket for more information.

In Phuket, both **Siam Safari Nature Tours** (tel: 0 7628 0116) and **Phuket Union Travel** (tel: 0 7622 5522) offer 2-day trips to Krabi. In Krabi Town, travel agents like Jungle Book (tel: 0 7561 1148) and **Songserm Travel** (tel: 0 7561 2665/6) are conveniently located. **Tourism Authority of Thailand** (tel: 0 7561 2740) has a small branch office on the river promenade.

Left: snorkelling at Similan
Above: a chicken-shaped island near Krabi

Krabi's Attractions

Krabi Province has four main areas of interest: the town, beaches, islands and the interior. With a population of 15,000, **Krabi Town** is located on the Krabi River with extensive mangrove forests on the opposite bank. You may wish to hire a long-tailed boat to do a spot of birdwatching in the mangrove canals, or visit the **Kanab Nam** limestone twin peaks with its huge cave hidden inside. Decent accommodation is available at hotels in Krabi. In the evenings, you can dine out at either of the two simple night markets. Krabi's beaches, notably, Ao Nang, Nopparat Thara, Rai Leh (both east and west) and Phra Nang, are located some distance from town but are easily accessed by road and also by boat.

The mangrove forests of Krabi have remained remarkably intact and are home to many types of fish, crabs, shrimps and shellfish. They are also important nesting grounds for hundreds of different bird species, as well as providing shelter for dugongs, monkeys, lizards and sea turtles. A visit to the mangroves is easily organised. Half-day boat tours to nearby estuaries can be booked in Krabi Town – or you can simply hire a boat at the Chao Fah pier. Bird species that frequent the mangrove areas include the white-bellied sea eagle and Ruddy Kingfisher, as well as the Mangrove Pitta, Masked Finfoot, rare Nordmanns Greenshank and the Great Knot. It may be a muddy experience, but to naturalists, the mangrove swamps are a paradise.

World-class Beaches

Ao Nang Beach, 15km (9 miles) by bus from town, is the most popular beach in the region, and also the most developed. The water is clear and not too deep, while there are easily-accessed coral reefs quite close inshore. Ao Nang is also the longest of Krabi's beaches, with a wide range of restaurants and accommodation to suit all budgets. Many people stay in Ao Nang

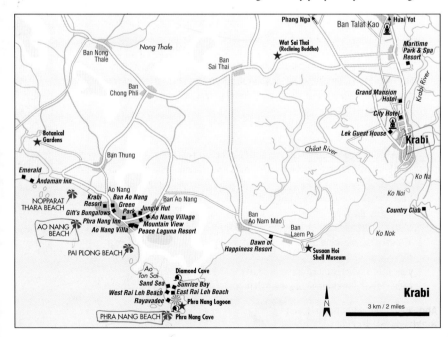

and take a long-tailed boat to Rai Leh and Phra Nang beaches 3km (2 miles) away on the cape of Laem Phra Nang. These two have been acclaimed as being among the most attractive in the world, their fine sands flanked by 200-m (650-ft) tall limestone outcrops. Properly speaking, **Rai Leh Beach** may be divided into two beaches, East and West. The former, **Rai Leh East**, is rather muddy at low tide, and people staying here tend to frequent **Rai Leh West**, which is sandier and generally more attractive.

In between the two Rai Leh beaches is **Phra Nang Beach**, beyond question the most beautiful beach in the Krabi region, and by any standards, one of the loveliest in Thailand. Named after a mythical princess called Phra Nang whom the locals believe lives here, the beach is made up of fine, soft and clean sand backed by tall limestone cliffs. If you visit the cave of **Tham Phra Nang Nok**, set in the limestone cliffs, you will see it is well-stocked with wooden phalluses: these are offerings to Phra Nang by local fishermen in the hope of ensuring good harvests. On the headland of Phra Nang beach is the luxurious **Rayavadee** (tel: 0 7562 0740; www.rayavadee.com) with its unobtrusive Thai-style pavilions.

Also well worth a visit is the **Nopparat Thara Beach**, just 3km (2 miles) northwest of Ao Nang. The name – which means 'Beach of the Nine-Jewelled Stream' – is derived from a small waterway that flows into the Andaman Sea at this point. The beach is around 2km (1¼ miles) long and forms part of the Hat Nopparat Thara – Ko Phi Phi National Marine Park *(Excursion 3)*, which provides the area with a degree of protection against environmental damage. There are a few government bungalows that visitors can stay in, as well as a number of small hotels, restaurants and bars, but on the whole it's a delightfully quiet destination with relatively few visitors.

Day Trips from Krabi

There are lots of interesting tours you can book from Krabi, such as a day-trip to **Ko Poda**, 6km (4 miles) offshore from Ao Nang. Poda is a windswept sandy island with one or two food shacks and superb clear waters for swimming and snorkelling. A 3-hour boat ride from Krabi Town takes you to **Ko Lanta** in the south of the province. The backdrop of the hills is gentler here, but with all 19 beaches flanking the west coast, it is very rainy during the southwest monsoon (May to November). The rest of the year it is a quieter alternative to Phuket, with budget to mid-range accommodation.

Above: stunning Phra Nang Beach
Right: Ko Poda island

Another interesting place to visit is the **Khao Phanom Bencha National Park**, which rises to 1,350m (4,430ft) and is clad in dense primary forest. This 500-sq km (190-sq mile) park located north of Krabi Town is home to a wide variety of wildlife. There are more than 30 mammal species, including the Asiatic black bear, the Malaysian sun bear and the rare clouded leopard, in addition to nearly 200 species of birds. There are two large waterfalls, **Huay To** and **Huay Sadeh**, both of which are best visited at the end of the rainy season. The former, in particular, is good for a dip, and makes a rewarding half-day trip from town.

Northwest of Krabi Town is **Thanboke Korani National Park**, which draws day-trippers who gaze in awe at the emerald river flowing out of a cave. Established as recently as 1991, this park includes a number of large caves, a botanical garden and several attractive waterfalls.

Just 7 km (4½ miles) north of Krabi Town is **Wat Sai Thai**. Home to a large 15-m (50-ft) Reclining Buddha concealed beneath an overhanging limestone cliff, this formerly active monastery still has a few monks in residence. The bell tower and some stone foundations are all that remain of the main temple building today, but it's worth visiting to see the Reclining Buddha and to enjoy the beautiful rural setting.

Another temple worth visiting is **Wat Tham Sua** (Tiger Cave Temple), located some 5km (3 miles) north of Krabi Town. It offers a hike up a 305-m (1,000-ft) staircase to see Buddha's footprint on top of a ridge. The view is breathtaking from the top. The temple is built into a cave set in a limestone cliff. Surrounded by *kuti*, which are stilted huts that monks live in, it is one of southern Thailand's best-known temples. The temple grounds are attractive, and there are two separate stairways leading to an eye-catching Kuan Yin image, known more commonly as the Chinese Goddess of Mercy, and to the reputed footprint of the Buddha. The climb to the latter, with over 1,200 steps, is quite hard going, so take your time if you're not in good shape.

Hot Springs and Waterfalls

About 30 minutes drive south of Krabi, the small town of **Klong Thom** is visited for its hot springs and trekking opportunities. The hot springs are suitable for bathing, while the local Tung Tieo Nature Trail also offers an attractive natural rock pool to cool off. The local temple, **Wat Khlong Thom**, has a small but rather esoteric museum displaying various trade goods such as beads, pots and weapons dating from the time when Khlong Thom was a stopover on the peninsular trade route between India and the South China Sea.

Finally, make time to visit the fascinating **Susaan Hoi** or Shell Fossil Cemetery, located about 17km (10 miles) west of Krabi, near Ban Laem Pho. Susaan Hoi is a 'shell graveyard' where fossilised shells dating back more than 75 million years have formed unusual stone piers which extend out into the sea.

Left: Kuan Yin image at the famous Wat Tham Sua

6. KHAO SOK NATIONAL PARK *(see map, p52)*

Situated in western Surat Thani Province, this 646-sq km (249-sq mile) park contains 65,000 hectares (161,000 acres) of dense primary rainforest, limestone cliffs, rivers, waterfalls, a lake and numerous trails.

Day trips from Phuket involve a 7.30am pick-up in a Land Rover for a 3-hour road journey to the mountainous park. On the way, stops may be made at the beach in Phang Nga and at Lampi Waterfall for a refreshing swim, so pack a swimsuit. Contact **Siam Safari Nature Tours** *(tel: 0 7628 0116; www.khaosok.com) for tour details.*

Conjoined with two other national parks, Kaeng Krung and Phang Nga, as well as Khlong Saen and Khlong Nakha wildlife sanctuaries, this extensive conservation area comprises the largest nature preserve in Thailand. **Khao Sok National Park** is home to a wide range of wildlife, including elephant, leopard, tiger, Malayan sun bear, serow, gaur, langur and banteng. Bird species are even more numerous with over 200 registered at present. Unfortunately, the Khao Sok tigers, currently believed to number less than 10, are still seriously threatened by poachers.

The park is also filled with a profusion of lianas, bamboo, rattan and giant tropical ferns. One particularly spectacular plant is the *Rafflesia*, the flower of which reaches 80cm (31 inches) in diameter, and is the largest bloom in the world. *Rafflesia* has no roots or leaves of its own and lives parasitically inside the roots of the liana. When the bud blooms in January, it emits a powerful smell, which attracts pollinating insects, but generally repels people.

Khao Sok National Park is best visited in the dry season (December to May); trails are less slippery and river crossings are certainly much easier. During this time of the year, camping is considered safe. During the wet season, however, visitors are more likely to see the larger mammals, which tend to stay near the reservoir and away from the jungle trails in the dry season.

On arrival at Khao Sok, organised tour visitors, accompanied by a guide, will trek for about 2 hours through fascinating primary rainforest that dates back millions of years or more. Halfway through the trek, coffee is served in specially cut bamboo cups. There are about 2 hours left for hiking in the forest – time enough to explore a cave and swim in a river.

Guests then have a hearty meal at one of the tree-house bungalows before the 2½-hour return trip to Phuket. If you're travelling on your own, there are guesthouses near the park entrance where you can spend the night, and which can also arrange guided tours to the main waterfalls and caves in the park. Leeches are common in many areas of the park, so it's best to wear closed shoes when hiking and apply copious amounts of insect repellent.

Right: strange but fascinating flora are found at Khao Sok National Park

Leisure *Activities*

SHOPPING

Phuket does not offer the same volume and variety of shopping outlets as you would find in Bangkok or Chiang Mai but the prospect of going on a major spending spree has improved over recent years with the arrival of larger shopping malls. There are a few local handicrafts but most gift items are imported from other regions of the country. If you plan to visit other parts of Thailand, spend your time enjoying Phuket and save your shopping for later.

Still, there are some good shopping opportunities in Phuket. Since the devaluation of the baht, the bargains even more enticing. And there is still scope to bargain.

Local Crafts

Also known by the sobriquet, 'Pearl of the South', Phuket lives up to its name as a producer of natural, cultured and artificial **pearls**. Made of an amalgam of lead and tin, **pewterware** is also a traditional craft here as tin is mostly mined locally. Steins, plates and other items are sold at prices lower than in other parts of the country.

Nang Thalung, or brightly-coloured **shadow puppets**, cut from buffalo hide, make excellent wall decorations and souvenirs as is batik. The south is a major batik centre, producing both ready-made clothes and fabric lengths. **Purses** and **bags** woven out of *yan lipao*, a fine locally-grown and dyed grass, are another good buy.

Regional Crafts

The crafts listed below are mainly produced in Chiang Mai and Northeastern Thailand.

Thai silk: This iridescent cloth has achieved world fame, and for good reason. It can be cut into beautiful dresses as well as pillowslips, scarves and ties. It is also sold by the metre.

Clothes: Phuket has a wide range of beach clothes and summer evening wear at very attractive prices. You could arrive with the barest wardrobe and find everything you need right here. Phuket artists produce beautiful T-shirts that make excellent gifts. Many shops and stalls in Patong's Soi Bangla and along Thawiwong Road sell good quality cotton T-shirts with prices from 150 baht up.

Wood: Images of gods, animals, precocious children, and betel nut boxes in a variety of finishes, are very popular. Shops also offer wooden furniture and will ship your purchases for you.

Gems and Jewellery: Thailand is the world's largest coloured gem cutting centre and has a huge jewellery industry, so prices are reasonable. I hesitate, however, to recommend specific shops. Countless visitors have told of being charged high prices for jewellery that has turned out to have a gold content less than stated, or a gem that is not of the quality advertised. If the shop provides a certificate of guarantee attesting to the quality of the item, then buy it. But even then, you may have trouble getting your money back if you discover that your purchase is a fake.

Baskets: Wicker and grasses are made into storage boxes, mats, tissue boxes and other practical household items.

Metal art objects: Bronze deities, characters from the *Ramakhien*, and animal and abstract figures are cast up to 2m (6.5ft) tall and clad in gleaming brass skins. Bronze is also crafted into cutlery sets while silver and gold are pounded into jewellery trinket, boxes and other decorative items.

Home decor items: Artificial flowers and fruits made of fabric and paper are virtually indistinguishable from fresh varieties. Burmese *kalaga* wall hangings – stuffed with cotton to create a bas-relief effect – and depicting gods,

Left: Thai silk comes in a rainbow of colours
Right: mask woodcarving

kings and mythical animals, are commonly found. Papier-mâché products make super gift and home decor items.

Lacquerware: These come in two varieties: gleaming gold and black, and matte red with black and/or green details. Items include ornate containers and trays, wooden figurines and other objects.

Ceramics: Most Thai ceramic items are produced in the north. These range from the jade-green glazed celadon pottery to earthenware, stoneware and Chinese blue-and-white items.

Leather: The items are prosaic enough – shoes, bags, wallets, attaché cases and belts – but the animals that have contributed their hides include snake, armadillo, lizard, crocodile, cow, frog and even chicken. Check your home country's import restrictions.

Umbrellas: Chiang Mai produces lovely umbrellas and fans made from silk or *sa* paper made from tree bark.

Charcoal portraits: Artists work from live sittings or photographs to create superb charcoal or oil portraits. A family photograph from home can be transformed into a painting. The price depends on size: a 40cm x 60cm (16in x 24in) charcoal portrait costs around 1,000 baht. There are several studios in Patong that offer this service.

Where to Shop

Central Festival (tel: 0 7629 1111) is Phuket's largest shopping centre. Located in Amphur Muang, the three-floor mall contains numerous shops, restaurants and a cinema. With the opening of its fourth floor, it will have a bowling alley as well.

Silk Master (tel: 0 7623 9060/2, daily 9am–6pm,), on the left at KM9 off H402, specialises in Thai silk but it also sells leather products, pewter, cotton, brass, bronze, batiks and 'elephant hide' shoes. Like all emporia, ignore the 'fixed price' signs and barter.

Thai Village (tel: 0 7621 4860/1, daily 10am–10pm), 1km (½ mile) off H402 at KM2.5. This has a wide range of items for sale. In addition, you can see artisans at work. The emphasis is on southern crafts, so you'll see more use here of sea shells, bamboo, coconut husks, rubber tree wood and batiks than at most other retailers.

Thai Style (tel: 0 7621 5980, daily 8am–7pm), on the right at KM9 off H402, is an up-market wood carving centre specialising in the Chiang Mai, Mandalay and Khmer styles. You will find mostly teak wood carvings, ranging from tabletop items at a few hundred baht, to furniture and wall murals for over 300,000 baht.

If you are interested in jewellery, you will find a handful of gem shops, including **World Gems**, and **Chai Dee Gems**, in Bangla Road near the Thawi Wong Road junction in Patong. Insist on a guarantee.

In Phuket Town, most of the better handicraft and souvenir shops are found along Rasda, Phang Nga, Yaowaraj (southern end) and Montri roads. The main shops are **Puk**, **Phuket Souvenir Centre**, **Nida**, **Rasda Souvenir** and **Land & Sea**. Two of these stand out: **Ban Boran Antiques** (39 Yaowaraj Road, tel: 0 7621 2473) has a limited but impressive collection of antiques, which are laid out almost like a museum. **Antique Arts** (68 Phang Nga Road, tel: 0 7621 3989) has a collection of exquisite Chinese porcelains, brass and lacquerware displayed in glass-fronted cabinets.

Above: bronzeware artisan at work
Right: Chiang Mai umbrellas

EATING OUT

One of the joys of a holiday in Phuket is the chance to savour its superb cuisine. Its waters are rich with crabs, tiger prawns, shrimp, mussels, squid and half a dozen varieties of fish, and its land abounds with fresh vegetables and fruits. Seafood, fresh from trawlers, and vegetables from the countryside are sped to kitchens to be turned into unforgettable dishes.

Phuket is best known for its giant spiny lobsters: huge, hard-shell beasts, which must be seen to be believed. Observe them live in tanks in front of restaurants on Patong's Thawiwong Road (the road parallel to the beach). Lobsters can weigh up to 3kg (7lbs), have bodies 35cm (13 in) long and antennae which are 60cm (24 in).

The island has always been known for its Thai cuisine but as its status as an international resort grows, more and more Asian and Continental restaurants are springing up to add variety to mealtimes.

Unlike many other holiday resorts, top class hotels and restaurants in Phuket never had a monopoly on good food. The island has always been known for its culinary discoveries in unpretentious settings – a lantern-lit seafood shack by the beach, or a Thai curry shop in the suburbs of town.

Most visitors prefer their seafood cooked Thai-style. Thai cooks rely on garlic, lemongrass, chillies, coriander, shrimp paste and dozens of herbs and spices, to impart a delicious flavour to their dishes. Among the favourites are *plamuuk phat kratiem prik thai* (squid fried with garlic and black pepper), *homok talay* (a seafood mousse made with chunks of fish and shellfish, smothered in coconut cream and wrapped in banana leaf), *tom yam kung* (a spicy soup of shrimps seasoned with lemon grass and served in a charcoal-heated tureen), or its cousin, *po tak* (the 'fisherman's net bursts') which blends half a dozen seafood items in a tangy broth. For variety, try *plaa chalam phat prio wan* (sweet and sour shark) or an exotic appetiser like deep-fried sea cicadas.

Desserts are a Thai speciality. Try coconut ice cream (ice cream *ka-thi*) and a host of other goodies with a base of coconut milk or vermicelli and incorporating sticky rice and luscious fruits.

For a refreshing drink, try chilled young coconuts; drink the juice, then scrape out and eat the tender young flesh. Coffee drinkers should sip the very strong Thai coffee flavoured with chicory. Tea drinkers will find the odd, orange-coloured Thai tea sticky sweet, but delicious. On a hot day, the Chinese prefer to drink a cup of hot, very thin tea, but never with ice, as they believe that ice is bad for the stomach.

Locally produced beers include Singha, Chang and Leo, as well as Tiger, and Heineken. Of the many Thai cane whiskeys, Sang Som is the most popular.

Above: spicy chicken noodle soup

Prices are usually clearly displayed on menus or signboards outside restaurants. A filling meal for one person without drinks is categorised as follows:

Inexpensive = less than 250 baht;
Moderate = 250–500 baht;
Expensive = over 500 baht.

Bang Thao

Puccini
Sheraton Grande Laguna
Tel: 0 7632 4101-7
Contemporary fine-dining Italian restaurant serving a variety of pizza, pasta, risotto and meat dishes along with a large selection of Italian wines. *Moderate*

Ruen Thai
Dusit Laguna Resort
Tel: 0 7632 4320
Central Royal Thai cuisine served by waitresses in Thai classical costumes to the accompaniment of *kim* (classical music). Romantic candlelit setting beside a lake. *Expensive*

Saffron
Banyan Tree Resort
Tel: 0 7632 4374
Middle Eastern and Asian cuisine served in lush surroundings on chic earthenware crockery. *Expensive*

Above: Thai sweets filled with bean paste
Right: a hotel coffee shop

Tatonka
Dusit Laguna entrance
Tel: 0 7632 4349
An open-air, Spanish-style bar with innovative fusion cuisine from around the world. Open in the evenings only. *Moderate*

Chalong

Jimmy's Lighthouse
Kata Road, Chalong Circle, Chalong Bay
Tel: 0 7628 0840
Breezy open-air seaside eatery. Inspired international and Thai food with daily specials from Italy to India. *Moderate*

Kan Eang 1
9/3 Chao Fa Road, Chalong Bay
Tel: 0 7638 1212, 7638 1323
Simple open-air restaurant on the waterfront. Popular with locals and tourists alike. Seafood dishes are a speciality. *Moderate*

Karon

Karon Café
33/76 Patak Road
Tel: 0 7639 6217
Busy, well-run Scandinavian-American restaurant serving free salad and soup with wholesome main course meals. Imported steaks and ribs a speciality. Good Thai selection too. Open all day. *Moderate*

Old Siam
Thavorn Palm Beach Hotel
Tel: 0 7639 6116, 7639 6552
Restaurant with an emphasis on royal Thai traditions. Nightly *kim* (classical music) performances and Thai dancing. *Moderate*

On the Rock
Marina Cottage
Tel: 0 7633 0625
Very popular small restaurant on the rocks overlooking Karon Bay. Strong on Thai food, seafood and international items. Reservations are advisable. *Moderate*

Phaitong
Patong-Karon Coast Road
Tel: 0 7628 6080
Seafood and international cuisine served in romantic tropical setting with superlative view overlooking Karon Beach. *Moderate*

Kata

Boathouse Wine & Grill
Mom Tri's Boathouse, Kata Beach
Tel: 0 7633 0015
Refined Thai and European dining on a romantic terrace overlooking the sea. Large wine selection and set menus available. Reservations are essential. *Expensive*

Islanders
6/3 Soi Tuey Ngam, Patak Road
Tel: 0 7633 0740
Busy open-air restaurant in south Kata. Seafood is the mainstay but Italian fare is also served. *Inexpensive–Moderate*

Kampong Kata Hill
112/2 Moo 4, Patak Road, Kata
Tel: 0 7633 0103
Unique Thai and seafood restaurant in a romantic open-air setting surrounded by Asian *objets d'art. Moderate*

Siri's Kitchen
111/11 Moo 2 Kata Centre
Tel: 0 7633 0580
Thai, Chinese and European cuisine by a chef who previously worked at Bangkok's The Oriental hotel. He recommends shark steak, clams and mussels with Franco-Italian crêpes for dessert. *Moderate*

Nai Harn

Regatta Bar & Grill
Le Royal Meridien Phuket Yacht Club
Tel: 0 7638 1156
There's a colonial feel to this exclusive but understated international and seafood restaurant in one of Phuket's best hotels. Specialist wine list. *Expensive*

Patong

Baan Rim Pa
100/7 Kalim Beach Road
Tel: 0 7634 0789, 7634 1768
Delightfully located romantic restaurant with views of Patong Bay. Refined central Thai dining by candlelight. Reservations are advisable. *Expensive*

Malee Seafood Village
Thawi Wong (Beach) Road,
Tel: 0 7634 0205
Busy outdoor seafood emporium in central Patong. The meal starts with a choice from one of the mouth-watering displays of seafood on ice. *Moderate*

Pizzeria Napoli
Soi Patong Post Office
Tel: 0 7634 0674
Indoor dining on a wide range of pizzas, pastas and other Italian specialities. Limited outside seating available. *Inexpensive*

The Royal Kitchen
Royal Paradise Hotel
70 Paradise Complex
Tel: 0 7634 0172
Chinese restaurant perched on top of a 25-storey hotel. Fabulous panoramic views of Patong. *Moderate*

Seafood No 4
104/32 Thaveenong Road, Soi Permpong
Tel: 0 7634 2319
Choose from a wide variety of seafood laid

out on beds of ice. Lobsters are displayed in huge plastic basins for customers to select. Choice of seafood cooked either Thai or European style. *Moderate*

Phuket Town

Ka Jok See
26 Takua Pa Road
Tel: 0 7621 7903
Intimate and delightful 'off-the-wall' Thai restaurant. Newspaper table covers, household antiques and a porch with verdant potted plants create a raffish feel underscored by jazz music. *Moderate*

Laem Thong
31–39 Chana Charoen Road
Tel: 0 7621 1269, 7622 4349
Large, urbane Chinese-Thai restaurant specialising in Thai seafood and Beijing cuisine. Lobster, oyster and suckling pig are its specialities. *Expensive*

Mala
5/72–73 Mae Luan Road
Tel: 0 7621 4201
Open-front restaurant decorated with vintage household artefacts. Tasty curries like *kaeng matsman kai* are made fresh daily. Try the *khao yam* or rice with *kapi* (a paste made of fermented shrimp). *Moderate*

Metropole Coffee Shop
Metropole Hotel, Montri Road
Tel: 0 7621 5050
Up-market but very good-value lunch venue with a bountiful buffet spread of Thai cuisine from four regions of the country. Prompt table service. Thai classical music plays in the background. *Moderate*

Thai Naan
16 Vichit Songkhram Road
Tel: 0 7622 6164
Mammoth teak-panelled Thai, Chinese and Japanese restaurant claiming to be the largest in South Thailand. The southern Thai set dinner, served 'khantoke' stye in the Srivichai Room and accompanied by classical Thai dancing and music, is highly recommended. *Moderate*

The Rooftop
Pearl Hotel, 42 Montri Road
Tel: 0 7621 1044
Excellent Cantonese restaurant on the top floor of the hotel. Popular with the local business community and locals who know where to find good food. Features live musical entertainment. *Expensive*

Tung-ka Café
Top of Khao Rang (Phuket Hill)
Tel: 0 7621 1500
Romantic open-air Thai restaurant with sweeping views of Phuket Town and the coast. Small selection of Japanese and Western dishes. Famed for its *nam prik kung siap* (dried prawn roasted on a stick). At its best by night with views of the town lit up below. *Moderate*

Surin

The Sundown Café
106/13 Surin Beach
Tel: 0 7627 0230
Delicious Tex-Mex food served in huge portions in a small café by the beach. Also home-made pizzas, pastas, ice creams and Margaritas. Rhythm and blues background music. Closed on Mondays. *Moderate*

NIGHTLIFE

Phuket's nightlife scene is nothing like Bangkok's or Pattaya's but it is certainly going in that direction. Phuket Town has Thai-style nightclubs which are more appealing to local than foreign tastes, and it has cinemas and a night market. As might be expected, Patong, the most developed of the resorts, offers the widest nightlife opportunities. Kata and Karon are now beginning to open up as well.

Nightlife in Phuket really centres on dining and what the Thais call *barbeers* – open-air bars with the bartenders inside, and the patrons sitting on stools arranged on the outside. The bars have hostesses to entertain and play video movies and music so loud that when several *barbeers* are clustered together, conversation is virtually impossible. Although there are no raunchy sex shows, like those found in Bangkok and Pattaya, Phuket no longer has a squeaky-clean atmosphere. 'Body massage' parlours are common in Patong and Phuket Town.

Hotels usually have cocktail bars where Filipino or Thai musicians entertain. Some hotels also screen in-house movies at their bars to keep customers glued to their seats.

Karon
Bars

Nightlife in Karon is comparatively low-key compared to Patong, but there are two separate bar areas, each with a number of small, friendly bars. These operations do tend to come and go, but some names that you might look out for are **Pink Paradise Bar** and **Thunder Bar** along Patak Road East (north Karon), and **Nakonnai** and **Valhalla** on Patak Road West (south Karon).

Ma Ma Bar
36/2 Patak Road
Tel: 0 7639 6812
A small, raucous bar that stays open well into the early hours.

Kata
Live Music
Easyriders
The Kata Centre
Specialises in the music of great legends

like Eric Clapton, played full tilt by Thai bands.

Bars
Bluefin Tavern
111/17 Taina Road, Kata-Karon headland
Tel: 0 7633 0856
Widely regarded as one of the best bars on Phuket, with a mix of locals and visitors.

Voodoo Pub
111-15 Kata Centre
Tel: 0 7633 0869
This psychedelically painted joint attracts many locals.

Jazz
The Boathouse Bar
Mom Tri's Boathouse, Kata Beach
Tel: 0 7633 0015
The island's best jazz sextet plays on Wednesday and Saturday evenings.

Patong

The main nightlife area in Patong is in the Bangla Road area. Entire lanes of *barbeers* packed with loud music and provocative hostesses are found at the **Bangla Centre**.

Bars
Alice Bar
98/4 Rachauthit Road
Tel: 0 7634 1194
One of the most popular bars on Patong's main strip.

Hard Rock
82/10 Bangla Road
Tel: 0 7634 1271
Not part of the international chain, but can play almost any rock song ever recorded from its vast collection.

Ned Kelly's
93/16 Bangla Road
Tel: 0 7634 0711
Excellent place for watching Patong's nightly spectacle.

Paradise Bar
Thawiwong Road next to the Holiday Inn
Reputedly Patong's longest running bar and still a favourite.

Left: deep-fried fish in 'three-flavoured' sauce

Go-Go Bars

Scantily clad dancers on a raised stage differentiate a go-go bar from an ordinary bar in Phuket. They are commonly regarded as the haunts of single males, but couples are welcome and will be treated with the usual Thai hospitality. Most go-go bars offer happy hours from 8–10pm.

Extasy
Soi Sunset, 50/51 Rachauthit Road
Tel: 0 7634 1510
One of the most popular go-go bars in Patong – with over 30 dancers nightly.

Rock Hard
82/51 Bangla Road
Tel: 0 7634 0409
One of Phuket's original go-go bars, it also advertises itself as Thailand's biggest. Popular with the US Navy when in town.

Live Music
Molly Malone's Irish Pub
88 Thawiwong Road
Tel: 0 7629 2771
This is the island's first Irish theme bar and a popular establishment in Phuket. While having a drink here, also try their fish and chips or the Irish stew. They also serve draft Guinness. A resident Irish rock band plays every night.

Otawa
100/7 Kalim Beach Road
Tel: 0 7634 4254
Apart from serving excellent sushi, there's some superb jazz sessions from the Raw Jazz Quartet, members of which have played with such jazz luminaries as Louis Armstrong and Dizzy Gillespie.

Pow Wow Pub
70/179-180 Royal Paradise Complex,
Moo 3 Rachautit Road
Tel: 0 7634 0756
safari@loxinfo.co.th
A theme pub that features live country and western music and entertainment nightly. Thai and Western food also served. Attracts a mixed crowd of both locals and foreigners.

Discos
Discos are very popular in Patong. They usually open around 11pm and charge a nominal entrance fee (redeemable for a drink).

Banana Disco
Thawiwong Road
Tel: 0 7634 0301
The oldest disco in Patong is a good place to catch the latest hits. There is also an attached open-air pub to relax in. The area is a well-known drop-off and pick-up point for hotel transportation.

Pasha
Soi Sunset
Tel: 0 7634 0174
Only really gets going around midnight, but once it does, this is the place to be seen. Plays mainly house and top 40 hits.

Safari Disco and Fun Pub
28 Sirirat Road, Patong Hill
Tel: 0 7634 1079
Located slightly south of central Patong on the road to Karon. Raucous and highly popular, they regularly feature live bands. Great fun after 11pm.

Star Club
Bangla Road
Tel: 0 7634 0525
This new incarnation of the former Shark Club is still the largest disco in Patpong.

Above: Patong night lights

Cabaret
Phuket Simon Cabaret
8 Sirirat Road, Patong Beach
Tel: 0 7634 2011
Holds three opulent transvestite stage-shows a night, two in low season. The innocuous and very entertaining 90-minute shows, with a cast of 80 'girls' cost 400–500 baht, depending on seating. The ticket price is inclusive of an alcoholic drink.

Thai Kickboxing
Vegas Beer Bar
51 Bangla Road
Tel: 0 7634 1633
If you have any interest in the Thai martial art, *muay thai*, then this is a great place to come. Bouts occur nightly between 9.30pm and 1am.

Phuket Town
Nightlife options in Phuket town are fewer than in Patong but some places can be relied on for a good time. The scene however attracts mainly locals.

Live Music
Jammin' Music Club
78/28 Bangkok Road
Tel: 0 7622 0189
A Caribbean-styled venue with live reggae, rock, R&B and alternative bands. Free shuttle service from the southern beaches.

Kon Thai
Opposite the Phuket Garden Hotel
Tel: 0 7621 7283
A mix of Thai and international musical styles. Famous for its Thai Country Rock, a form supposedly influenced by the American South. Daily 9pm–2am.

Timber'n Rock
118/1 Yaowaraj Road
Tel: 0 7621 1839
Local guitarist, Boonkirt performs nightly from 10pm with his band, *Heaven*. Attracts a big following with the local girls. Daily 8pm–2am.

Coffee Shops
For something with a local flavour, try the coffee-shops – highly popular with Thais. Attractive, usually female, singers alternate between playing host and singing winsome Thai pop songs on stage. It's more pleasing to the eye than the ear generally but go just for the fun of it. Food and drinks are reasonably priced.

Bua Luang
6 Padiphat Road
Tel: 0 7621 3167
Probably the most popular coffee shop in town. If you enjoy a particular singer, why not present him or her with a flower garland – you'll see flower garland sellers walking around the place.

Massage
Grand Plaza Massage
23 Tilok Uthit 1 Road
Tel: 0 7621 4921/5
A large parlour covering all forms of massage. Mon–Fri 2pm–midnight; Sat–Sun noon–midnight.

Pearl Massage
Pearl Hotel, Montri Road
Tel: 0 7621 1044
Offers a variety of massage styles. Traditional Thai massage can be very relaxing but also a bit painful. Don't be afraid to tell the masseuse to ease off if your limbs feel as though they may be twisted permanently!

Thai Kickboxing
Phuket Boxing Stadium
Phuket Road, Phuket Town
Tel: 0 7639 6591
Thai boxing differs from international-style boxing by allowing the combatants to use feet, knees, fists and elbows. The action is fast and furious, and betting takes place on the sidelines. Fridays only, 8pm.

Above: Thai boxers in action

OUTDOOR ACTIVITIES

Watersports

Patong Beach offers the widest range of water sports. Karon has more facilities than Kata, but neither compares with what Patong has. Although hotels provide limited facilities on their own private coves, it is mainly the local beach boys who rent out privately owned equipment for a wider range of watersports activities. They set their own prices but can be bargained down. Prices are further whittled down during the monsoon season when tourist numbers drop. The following price guide applies to the high season.

Windsurfing charges vary from 300 baht per hour to around 600 baht for half a day, and a free rudimentary lesson is offered with the rental fee.

Surfing beaches are found at Karon and Kalim on the northern end of Patong. Surfboards rent for about 100 baht per hour and the best time to surf is during the rainy season (May–November) when the waves pick up.

Catamarans generally rent for around 300–500 baht per hour, and if you don't sail,

hire someone for a small fee to take you out.

Parasailing is available on most beaches. It requires you to be strapped to a parachute and towed aloft by a powerboat for a 5-minute ride high over the bay. Be warned though, that this is not the safest sport in the world; riders have experienced bone-jarring drops on the beach. Check first to ensure the wind is not too strong and that the boat driver is experienced.

Jet-skis (600 baht per half hour) are popular, but the number of accident victims for this sport is rising. The unstable scooters sometimes flip on waves or their riders clothesline themselves on anchor ropes. Because they are unsafe and noisy, and because their operators invade the swimming areas in search of customers, some hotels have tried to have them banned.

Sea kayaks are a growing and very welcome alternative to jet-skis. Rental prices vary wildly from beach to beach and vendor to vendor, but plan on paying about half of what a jet-ski would cost.

Snorkelling

The only good places to snorkel in Phuket are on Kata Yai and Kata Noi beaches; otherwise, head further afield to Phi Phi or the Similan islands *(see Excursions 3 and 4)*. Corals and barnacles are very sharp and can cut deeply, so treat cuts immediately with disinfectant before they fester.

Another menace to snorkellers are sea urchins, and there are lots of them lurking in the corals. They look like dark maroon pincushions with iridescent orange and blue eyes. Step on one and you drive a poisonous spine into your foot, causing it to throb and ache for a long time. The traditional village treatment is to pound the embedded spine with stones to break it up. Someone then urinates into a coconut and the victim immerses the injured foot, the uric acid diluting the poison. If you find this remedy extreme, try the one most doctors recommend: go to a hospital.

Scuba Diving

The islands around Phuket and the distant Similans provide some of Southeast Asia's finest diving spots. The best time to dive is between December and April when the

Above: parasailing is fun – but has its share of danger

weather is fine, the seas are calm and underwater visibility is at its best. Many dive shops in Patong offer comprehensive courses that lead to internationally recognized PADI or NAUI open-water certification. Everything from introductory and open water dive certification to advanced diver and dive-master courses, is offered by dive shops. Shop around for the right price, and an experienced instructor who speaks your own language. Although competition keeps prices down, the cost alone shouldn't be the main deciding factor when choosing a dive course. It is worth paying an extra few hundred baht to go with a reliable and safe operator. The difference shows in the quality of instruction and equipment used.

Diving trip departures are usually guaranteed and no minimum number of participants is required. Dive prices are normally inclusive of the boat trip, tanks and weight belt only. All other equipment can be rented from the dive shops. Many operators now offer 'live aboard' trips to the Similan and Surin islands, Burma Banks, and the Mergui Archipelago. This means sleeping for 2–7 nights on board vessels varying from crudely converted fishing boats to comfortable boats with air-conditioned cabins. This option allows more dives per day and access to pristine underwater conditions. It also gives scope to explore remote beaches, sometimes with sea gypsy communities, notably in Surin and the Mergui islands.

The 'live aboard' option costs around 3,000–6,000 baht per person per day, inclusive of meals, accommodation, equipment and dive guides. The following dive operators are recommended:

Dive Asia
24 Karon Road, Kata Beach
Tel: 0 7633 0598
www.diveasia.com

Fantasea Divers
43/20 Moo 5, Viset Road, Chalong Bay
Tel: 0 7628 1388
www.fantasea.net

Marina Divers
45 Karon Road, Karon Beach
Tel: 0 7633 0272
www.marinadivers.com

Deep Sea Fishing

The waters off Phuket offer numerous challenges to deep-sea fishermen. Sailfish, barracuda, albacore, marlin, wahoo, tuna and king mackerel are just a few of the many varieties found. The average day trip runs 2,000 to 2,500 baht per person.

Aloha Tours
44/1 Viset Road, Chalong Bay
Tel: 0 7638 1215
With a number of deep sea fishing boats in their fleet, and experienced crew members manning all of them, a day's fishing with Aloha Tours can be a lot of fun, even for the complete novice.

Phuket Sportfishing Centre
Tel: 0 7621 4713
Shark fishing is their speciality; a boat is specially outfitted to deal with the rigours of hauling these big fish in.

Thai Fishing Guide
16/2 Moo 3 Soi Par Lai, Chalong
Tel: 0 7634 3024
Offer fresh- and salt-water fishing trips for first-time and experienced anglers.

Cruises

If you have the time and the money, a cruise on the waters of the Andaman Sea can be the experience of a lifetime. I suggest two itineraries: a northern route, which includes the Similan and Surin islands, and a more intense southern route which includes Racha, Phi Phi, Phang Nga Bay, the assorted Trang islands and the Tarutao group.

Above: diving lesson in progress

South East Asia Liveaboards
Patong Beach Road, Patong
Tel: 0 7634 0406
www.sealiveaboards.com
It runs several boats, including a 15.5-m (51-ft) trimaran called *Wanderlust* that holds eight passengers comfortably.

Thai Marine Leisure
Phuket Boat Lagoon, 20/7-8 Thepkasatri Road
Tel: 0 7623 9111
www.thaimarine.com
Reputable company that promises comfortable cruising in the Andaman Sea, with a fully qualified crew and the chance to do some big game fishing. All accommodation on board is on a twin-share basis.

Sunsail
Phuket Boat Lagoon, 22/1 Thepkasatri Road
Tel: 0 7623 9057
www.sunsail.com
Luxurious yachts can be chartered with or without a skipper.

Golf
Laguna Phuket Golf Club
393 Moo 1 Srioontorn, Bang Thao Bay
Tel: 0 7632 4374
A particularly challenging course, even for the best golfers; the par 3, 11th hole is especially tricky.

Blue Canyon Country Club
165 Moo 1 Thepkasatri Road, Thalang
Tel: 0 7632 8088
e-mail: golf@bluecanyonclub.com
Truly one of Asia's most spectacular golf courses with numerous awards to prove it. Has plenty of water hazards.

Phuket Country Club
80/1 Vichet Songkhram Road, Kathu
Tel: 0 7632 1039
Set amidst rolling hills. Across the road from the club is a driving range open daily, 7am–7.30pm.

Shooting
Phuket Shooting Range
82/2 Patak Road
Tel: 0 7638 1667
Open daily 9am–6pm and offers recreational rifle and pistol shooting.

Horse Riding
Phuket Laguna Riding Club
394 Moo 1, Bang Thao Beach (in front of Dusit Laguna Hotel)
Tel: 0 7632 4199
Riders are accompanied by an instructor through the fields, to the beach and back. Morning rides into the jungles are also offered. During the dry season, the owners lead 2-hour trips into the hills.

Above: the calm waters around Phuket are ideal for boat trips

CALENDAR OF EVENTS

Plan your visit to coincide with one of these Thai festivals. Thais celebrate even their religious holidays with gusto and invite the visitor to join in. Precise dates for many of the festivals and holidays may vary from year to year, as these are regulated by the lunar calendar. Check with the Phuket office of Tourism Authority of Thailand *(see page 90)*.

February

Magha Puja celebrates the gathering of 1,200 disciples to hear the Buddha preach. In the evening when the full moon rises, Buddhists gather at temples to honour him. Wat Chalong has an especially beautiful ceremony.

April

Songkran (April 13–15), the traditional Thai New Year, finds the Thais at their boisterous best. One blesses friends by sprinkling water on them, which soon develops into a full-scale war with ample dousings.
Turtle Release Festival (April 13) is the auspicious day when young turtles are released into the sea in a grand ceremony at Nai Yang Beach.

May

Visakha Puja commemorates Buddha's birth, enlightenment and death with elaborate temple ceremonies.
Loy Rua is a Chao Lay or Sea Gypsy festival held between the 13th–15th of the sixth and eleventh Thai lunar months, to mark the beginning and end of the monsoon season. Fishermen build 2½-m (8-ft) long model boats of bamboo and fill them with models of weapons as well as strands of hair, fingernail clippings and other items where bad luck is believed to reside.

July

Asalaha Puja commemorates Buddha's first sermon to his first five disciples.

September

Chinese Moon Festival is celebrated on the full moon night of the eighth lunar month. The moon goddess is honoured with shrines laden with fruit, incense and candles. It is a lovely festival with lanterns of all shapes and sizes lit up. Luscious moon cakes are sold, filled with nuts and salted eggs.

October

Vegetarian Festival is a Chinese celebration which runs from the 1st–9th of the ninth lunar month. There are daily processions through the streets but its most salient features are gruesome tests of devotion. Devotees enter trances and perform feats of daring, including climbing ladders with rungs made of knives, and piercing skewers and spears through cheeks and tongues.

November

Patong Carnival includes a Miss Patong contest, procession and ice-carving contest.
Loy Krathong (full moon day) is the most beautiful of Thai celebrations. As the full moon rises, Thais fill tiny floral floats with candles and incense and launch them into the rivers, canals, ponds and the sea to wash away sins and bless love affairs.
Buddhist Temple Fairs (November through February) are held during the cool season to raise money for temple repairs. In the evening, villagers gather to enjoy local drama troupes, carnival rides, and patronise booths selling farm produce. Ask at your hotel if one is being held nearby.

December

Phuket King's Cup Regatta is a week of races on Nai Harn Beach. The event has become a fixture on international yachting calendars, with the bay at Nai Harn transformed by a kaleidoscope of rainbow-coloured spinnakers from around the world.

Right: Phuket's Vegetarian Festival in October is not for the weak of heart

Practical
Information

GETTING THERE

By Air

Although airlines now fly directly to Phuket from Europe, Singapore and Hong Kong without Bangkok as an intermediate stop, the majority of travellers to Phuket step off daily flights from Bangkok.

Thailand's national carrier, **Thai Airways International** (THAI) (www.thaiair.com), offers several non-stop daily flights to and from Bangkok and one daily non-stop to and from Chiang Mai. Thai Airways International also flies non-stop between Phuket and Kuala Lumpur; Singapore; Hong Kong; Taipei; and Frankfurt.

Singapore Airlines (www.singapore air.com) and **Silk Air** (www.silkair.com) operate daily non-stop flights from Singapore and **Lauda Air** (www.laudaair. com) flies from Vienna via Bangkok. Numerous charter airlines fly in package tourists from November to April.

Both **Phuket Air** and **Bangkok Airways** (www.bangkokair.com) have daily flights from Bangkok to Krabi. From Phuket, **Bangkok Airways** flies daily to the island of Ko Samui as well as to Bangkok.

By Sea

Luxury liners from around the world occasionally stop in Phuket as part of their cruises to the region. The *SuperStar Gemini* from Singapore docks at the island once weekly.

TRAVEL ESSENTIALS

When to Visit

Phuket enjoys essentially hot summers (March–June) and mild winters (mid-November through mid-February). During the monsoon season (May–October), the rain generally falls only in the late afternoon, with clear weather the rest of the day and stunning sunsets. The best months are

November through February, but avoid Christmas/New Year and the Chinese Lunar New Year periods when hotels are fully booked despite hefty surcharges.

In the hot season, afternoon temperatures can rise to 30–34°C (86–93°F) but are tempered by cool breezes and dip to tolerable levels at night. Temperatures range from a daytime high of 34°C (93°F) in the hot season to a nighttime low of 21°C (70°F) in the cool season. The water temperature never drops below 20°C (68°F).

Visas and Passports

Visitors from many countries, including the UK and US, are issued 30-day entry permits, free, on arrival. Tourist visas valid for 60 days are available outside the country, depending on one's nationality. Check with a Thai embassy or consulate in your country before departure.

Tourist visas can usually be extended at the Immigration Division at the eastern end of Phuket Road in Saphan Hin (tel: 0 7621 2108; Mon–Fri, 8.30am–noon, 1–4.30pm), before the visa's expiration date. The 30-day entry permits can usually be extended, for a fee of 1,900 baht, for up to 10 days.

Check www.thaivisa.com for details on visa application and consulate locations.

Customs

Thailand prohibits the import of firearms and ammunition, pornographic materials, chemicals, and drugs. Cash imports of over $10,000 must be declared.

Left: beach huts near Ao Nang, Krabi
Right: "cattle crossing"

Vaccinations

Although the threat from cholera, polio and typhoid is minimal and inoculations are no longer required for entry into Thailand, vaccinations are suggested. Smallpox is no longer a threat.

Malaria is confined to the jungle areas on some parts of the mainland; if venturing to such places, a course of anti-malaria prophylaxis before arriving and during the stay is advised.

Certificates indicating recent inoculation against yellow fever may be requested at immigration checkpoints from visitors arriving from infected areas of the world. Rabies is prevalent but the chances of getting bitten are small.

Clothing

Clothing is casual; suits are virtually unknown. Think 'summertime' no matter what season you arrive. Natural fibres and blends are preferable to synthetics, as they breathe well in the humid air. Phuket's vendors sell stylish beach outfits.

The exceptions to the liberal clothing rule are Buddhist temples and Muslim mosques where a dress code is mandatory. In these places, shorts and singlets for men or sleeveless blouses for women are frowned upon. Shoes must be removed upon entering both temples and mosques, so sandals or slip-ons are handy.

You need a sturdy pair of leather shoes or running shoes if you plan to motorcycle around the island.

While malaria is not a problem in Phuket, dengue fever is, especially during the monsoon season from May to October. Carrying a bottle of mosquito repellant for the evenings and mornings is a good idea, as is wearing a long-sleeved shirt and pants. The mosquito is most active at dawn and dusk.

Electricity

Electricity is rated at 220 volts, 50 cycles. Both flat- and round-pronged plugs are used.

Time Zone

Phuket, like the rest of Thailand, is 7 hours ahead of GMT.

GETTING ACQUAINTED

Geography

The island of Phuket, surrounded by the Andaman Sea, is located 890km (550 miles) or a 70-minute flight south of Bangkok on Thailand's western coast. Measuring 49km (30 miles) long and 21km (13 miles) wide, and covering a total area of 587sq km (225sq miles), it is approximately the size of Singapore. Draped around it like a pearl necklace are an additional 70sq km (27sq miles) of islands.

Resembling the serrated shape of one of the seashells for which it is famous for, the

eastern shore was once the bank of a flooded river. Like the islands in Phang Nga Bay, the coastline on this side comprises limestone shoals and virtually no sandy beaches.

By contrast, the western coastline is granite-sculpted by the waves into a series of 16 coves carpeted in powdery white sand.

The island is surprisingly hilly with several peaks rising to 500m (1,640ft). Eleven percent of the interior is forested, including some primary rainforest found in the centre of the island.

Government and Economy

Thailand is a constitutional monarchy with power vested in an elected parliament and a senate appointed by the king from civilian and military officials. The executive branch consists of a coalition of political parties and a prime minister, who in turn rules through a cabinet. There is an independent judiciary.

Thailand enjoys a vigorous free-enterprise economy. Tourism is the principal foreign exchange earner, followed by agricultural produce and commodities. In the late 1980s, Thailand embarked on an ambitious programme of industralisation, which has transformed the countryside and recorded annual GNP growth rates as high as 13 percent. It has a well-developed telecommunications, transport and electricity infrastructure. With rapid growth, however, all these basic services are now under considerable pressure. Bangkok's congested roads are testimony to this. Thailand's economy took a sharp downturn in mid-1997 and the country is now fighting its way back to recovery.

Religion

About 73 percent of Phuket's population is Theravada Buddhist, 23 percent Muslim, and 3 percent Christian.

How Not to Offend

Thais regard the Royal Family with genuine reverence and react strongly to ill-considered remarks. They will not tolerate a refusal to stand for the Royal Anthem before the start of a movie.

Show similar respect towards Buddhist images, temples or monks. Thais take a dim view of men or women wearing shorts and sleeveless tops when visiting temples. Leave beachwear for the beach; dress appropriately even if the sun is threatening to bake you.

Temples and Chinese shrines are open to all visitors. There are no fixed opening hours but are generally open from 8am–6pm. They do not charge admission fees, but a small donation of 10 baht to cover maintenance or restoration costs would be appreciated. Remove your shoes before entering a Buddhist temple or a Taoist shrine.

You may photograph monks, temples, images and Buddhist ceremonies, but women should avoid touching a monk, even accidentally. This is because a monk's vow of chastity prohibits him from touching a woman, even his mother.

Similar respect should be shown towards Muslim religious sites. Foreigners are allowed into mosques but if a Muslim waves you away, just go. As a mark of respect, visitors should remove their shoes before entering a mosque and women should cover their heads with a shawl or a scarf.

The Thai greeting and farewell is 'Sawasdee'. It is said while raising the hands in a prayer-like gesture with the fingertips touching the nose, and by slightly bowing the upper portion of the body. It is an easy greeting to master and will earn you smiles wherever you go.

Thais believe in personal cleanliness. Even the poorest among them bathe daily and are dressed neatly and cleanly. They believe that the head is the fount of wisdom and all parts of the body from head down are progressively unclean. It is, therefore, an insult to touch someone on the head and to point one's feet at, or step over, a person.

Population

Phuket has a population of 300,000 people, 82,000 of whom live in Phuket Town in the south central part of the island. The rest of the population is concentrated in towns of no more than 3,000–5,000 people, and in villages or houses scattered in the rubber plantations and fields.

Money Matters
Currency

The Thai baht, is divided into 100 satang. Banknote denominations include 1,000B,

Left: palm trees, beaches and hills are part of Phuket's landscape

500B, 100B, 50B, 20B and 10B. There are 10B, 5B, 1B, 50-satang and 25-satang coins. Currently the baht fluctuates between 39 and 42 to the US dollar. For daily rates, check the *Bangkok Post* or *The Nation* newspapers. Government rates are also posted at banks and exchange kiosks. There is no currency black market.

Credit Cards
American Express, Diners Club, MasterCard and Visa are widely accepted in Phuket. Expect a surcharge of between 3 and 5 percent on their use at some outlets.

Cash Machines
Visa and MasterCard can be used to get cash advances at Kasikornbank, Siam Commercial Bank and Thai Military Bank. American Express cardholders should obtain cash advances from Bangkok Bank at 22 Phang-Nga Road (tel: 0 7621 1292/5).

Tipping
A 10 percent service charge is added to the bill at expensive restaurants but a small gratuity will be appreciated. In ordinary restaurants, a tip of 10 to 15 percent will be welcomed. There is no tipping in noodle shops or for street vendors. Room boys and chamber maids should be tipped but will not be offended if they are not. Taxi and bus drivers are not tipped.

Money Changers
Exchange rates are more favourable for travellers' cheques than for cash; hotels generally give poor rates. Change money at the small kiosks operated by major banks. They are found at Patong, Kata, Karon beaches and Phuket Town. Kiosks are normally open from 8.30am–8pm. Banks are open 8.30am–3.30pm.

Airport Tax
The airport tax for passengers departing on international flights is 500 baht. The tax for passengers departing for destinations within Thailand is 40 baht.

GETTING AROUND

From the Airport
Located on the northern end of the island, the airport is a 30-km (18-mile) or 45-minute drive from Phuket Town. As local bus services are infrequent, passengers must travel by one of the following means listed here.

Many of the major hotels have their own limousines to ferry guests with reservations (you can make a reservation at the airport) to their premises. They charge up to 600 baht per car.

Thai Airways International (THAI) operates a mini-van service between the airport and its Phuket Town office on Ranong Road for 100 baht, and to Patong, Kata or Karon beaches for 150 baht per passenger.

THAI Ground Services also offers air-conditioned limousines to each beach.

Car Rental
Cars and jeeps can be rented at a number of locations. A valid international or national driving license is all that's required. They may ask to photocopy your passport.

Reliable operators like Hertz, Avis, Budget and Via include insurance. Cheaper jeep rentals off the beachfront at Patong, Karon and Kata have no insurance cover. If you damage the vehicle you will have to pay an inflated repair fee. Always check the state of the vehicle before renting, and get the rental agent to acknowledge any scratches/deficiencies in the vehicle before setting off. Reliable companies will deliver the vehicle

Above: three-wheeled *tuk tuk*

to you, especially if you rent for two or more days. Day rentals are for 24 hours.

Avis: Phuket airport (tel: 0 7632 7358); Le Meridien Phuket (tel: 0 7634 0480/5); Laguna Beach Club (tel: 0 7632 4352)
Hertz: tel: 0 7632 8545
Budget: tel: 0 7620 5396/7 (airport)
Via: tel: 0 7634 1660 (Patong)
Pure: tel: 0 7621 1002 (Phuket Town)

Bus

Picturesque wooden buses ply regular routes. If you are not in a big hurry, they are a great way to get around. They leave every 30 minutes between 8am and 6pm from Phuket Town market for all beaches except Rawai and Nai Harn. Buses to Rawai and Nai Harn leave from the traffic circle on Bangkok Road. Return journeys from the beaches to the towns are also available from 8am–6pm.

Buses also prowl the roads in search of passengers. It is easy to flag one down.

Tuk-Tuks and Motorcycle Taxis

Tuk-tuks – small, four wheeled red vans – operate between Patong and Karon/Kata for up to 200 baht, depending on distance. In Phuket Town they charge 15–20 baht per person, regardless of distance covered within town.

Motorcycle taxis leave from the market on Ranong Road. Drivers in maroon vests convey the passenger on the backs of their motorcycles anywhere downtown for 10–20 baht per ride.

Mountain Bike Rental

Singletrak (tel: 0 7627 0936), outside the Dusit Laguna complex, offer bikes for 400 baht per day or 2,000 baht per week. **Tropical Trails** (tel: 0 7626 3239) charge around the same price with discounts for longer rentals. Bike rentals usually require a deposit of 1,000 baht and a photocopy of your passport. Rentals should include helmet, water bottle and a lock.

Motorcycle Rental

When you rent a motorcycle, you must surrender your passport for the duration of the rental period, so it is a good idea to change money first.

Motorcycles in Phuket range in size from small 90cc models like Honda Dream and

similar brands to giant 750cc behemoths. The majority are 125cc trail bikes, which are sufficient to climb the island's hills. Several rental outlets can be found on Rasada Road in Phuket Town.

Pure Car Rent, 75 Rasada Road, tel: 0 7621 1002. Honda Dream 100cc bikes for 150–200 baht per day, depending on demand. **Patong Big Bike**, 39/18–20 Rachautit Road, tel: 0 7634 0380. Bikes from 200cc to 1500cc.

Motorcycle rentals do not provide insurance so you are left to foot the bill if you damage the machine. The amount you pay for repairs will be at the owner's discretion, so drive cautiously and always wear a helmet. Just because the helmet law is only partially enforced by the police, don't try to get away with it. Violators, especially in town, are liable to spot fines. Ironically, police tend to overlook enforcement after dark when there is an even greater chance of an accident. Drink driving is widespread in Phuket. Remember Thais drive on the left-hand side of the road.

Be Warned: The number of travellers who have never handled a motorcycle before arriving in Phuket, but who try to learn during their holiday, is legion. So, too, is the number of traffic fatalities involving foreigners. On average, Vajira Hospital's intensive care unit admits 17 people injured from motorcycle accidents every day. Every day one of these people dies, and on average, at least one tourist dies every week.

HOURS AND HOLIDAYS

Business Hours

Banks are open Monday–Friday 8.30am–3.30pm. Bank-operated kiosks cum money changers vary their hours, opening at 8.30am or 9.30am and closing at 8pm, seven days a week.

Government offices are generally only open 8.30am–noon, and 1pm–4.30pm Monday–Friday.

Most hotels sell stamps at the reception desks or gift shops, and will also post letters and postcards. Shops, restaurants, and pharmacies stay open seven days a week, many until 10pm.

Public Holidays

New Year's Day: January 1
Magha Puja: February (full moon day)
Chakri Day: April 6
Songkran: April 13
Labour Day: May 1
Coronation Day: May 5
Visakha Puja: May (full moon day)
Asalaha Puja: July (full moon day)
HM the Queen's Birthday: August 12
Chulalongkorn Day: October 23
HM the King's Birthday: December 5
Constitution Day: December 10
New Year's Eve: December 31

ACCOMMODATION

The following are a selection of the more than 150 hotels in Phuket. Most have swimming pools, air-conditioned rooms and a variety of restaurants, and are completely self-contained. Price categories – based on published rates – for a standard double room are as follows:

$ = under 2,000 baht;
$$ = 3,000–4,000 baht;
$$$ = 4,000–5,000 baht;
$$$$ = above 6,000 baht.

Add 10 percent service charge and 7 percent tax to the prices. Note: prices fall by 30–50 percent in the low season.

Bang Thao Bay

The Banyan Tree
33 Moo 4, Srisoonthorn Road
Choeng Thalay District
Tel: 0 7632 4374; Fax: 0 7632 4375
www.banyantree.com/phuket
Individual, luxurious bungalows encircling a larger lagoon; some are garden bungalows; the more expensive ones have private outdoor pools. Full range of spa facilities. Low-key and luxurious and has won several international awards. The perfect getaway for honeymooners. *$$$$*

Dusit Laguna
390 Srisoonthorn Road
Choeng Thalay District
Tel: 0 7632 4320/32; Fax: 0 7632 4174
www.dusit-laguna.com
Part of the Dusit chain of deluxe hotels in Thailand, this five-star resort reflects its Thai heritage, apparent in its decor, staff apparel and the acclaimed Ruen Thai restaurant. However, the broad and sweeping Bang Thao Bay is exposed and it is unsafe to swim in the monsoon season. *$$$*

Laguna Beach Resort
Choeng Thalay District
Tel: 0 7632 4352; Fax: 0 7632 4353
www.lagunabeach-resort.com

Above: the Sheraton Grand Laguna

Sports-inclined resort with first-rate tuition in tennis, squash, archery and watersports. Friendly atmosphere for the young and active 'hands-on' crowd. Attractive swimming pool with Khmer-stone design and water slide. *$$$*

Sheraton Grande Laguna
Choeng Thalay District
Tel: 0 7632 4101/7; Fax: 0 7632 4108
www.sheraton.phuket.com
A 341-room deluxe hotel built around fresh water lagoons reclaimed from an old tin mining site. Numerous dining outlets. The star attraction is the unique winding swimming pool with piped-in music underwater. *$$$$*

Karon
Crowne Plaza Karon Beach
36/4 Patak Road
Tel: 0 7639 6139/48; Fax: 0 7639 6122
www.ichotelsgroup.com
Large, locally run resort in the the quiet part of Karon Beach. Facilities include tennis courts, gym, pool and tour desk. *$$–$$$*

Hilton Phuket Arcadia Resort & Spa
333 Karon Beach
Tel: 0 7639 6433/41; Fax: 0 7639 6136
www.hilton.com
Modern hotel with a recently-built new wing. Large rooms and a swimming pool. A hotel popular with Asian tourists. Lively disco nightly. *$$$$*

Marina Phuket Resort
47 Patak Road
Tel: 0 7633 0625; Fax: 0 7633 0516
www.marinaphuket.com
Thai-style cottages exquisitely landscaped into a hilly coconut plantation. There are also two excellent restaurants at the cottages: Sala Thai (offering mostly central Thai cuisine) and On the Rock (mostly seafood). *$$*

Kata
Club Med Phuket
7/3 Patak Road
Tel: 0 7633 0455; Fax: 0 7633 0461
www.clubmed.com
Large family-style resort in front of central Kata Beach. Caters to the young-at-heart, with lots and lots of organised activities.

Excellent French and international cuisine. *$$$*

Kata Beach Resort
1 Pakbang Road
Tel: 0 7633 0530/4; Fax: 0 7633 0128
www.katagroup.com
Well-appointed, large hotel-style resort on the south end of Kata Bay. Each of the 273 rooms has a balcony, a safe, and tea/coffee-maker. Known for its restaurants, particularly Silk Road (French) and Peppino's (Italian). *$$*

Mom Tri's Boathouse & Villa Royale
2/2 Patak Road
Tel: 0 7633 0015/7; Fax: 0 7633 0561
www.boathousephuket.com
Situated on the quiet end of Kata, this small and elegant beachfront 'boutique' hotel prides itself on attentive and personalised service. Main building built in the Ayutthaya-style, with steep sloping roofs. Famous for its sophisticated Boathouse Wine & Grill restaurant. Recently, the architect's own villa, perched on a forested headland overlooking the sea, has been converted into six luxurious suites and 12 deluxe studios. *$$$–$$$$*

Kata Noi
Kata Thani Hotel & Beach Resort
3/24 Patak Road
Tel: 0 7633 0124/6; Fax: 0 7633 0127
www.katathani.com
A four-star property with 433 rooms. Located on quiet Kata Noi where guests get pretty much the run of the stunning beach. Four swimming pools and full facilities. Five restaurants, serving seafood, German, Brazilian, Italian and Asian fare, plus a coffeehouse. *$$$*

Mai Khao
JW Marriott Phuket Resort & Spa
231, Moo 3, Mai Khao
Tel: 0 7633 8000; Fax: 0 7634 8348
www.marriotthotels.com
A five-star property with 265 oversized rooms, it is the only hotel on remote Mai Khao Beach. Set in sprawling landscaped gardens, the low-rise resort is just adjacent to a national park and a turtle nesting sanctuary. Full facilities including a spa and three restaurants. *$$$$*

Nai Harn

Le Royal Meridien Phuket Yacht Club
23/3 Viset Road
Tel: 0 7634 0480; Fax: 0 7634 0479
www.lemeridien.com
A luxury hotel popular with the yachting fraternity, particularly during the King's Cup Regatta in early December. Reputed for its service and breathtaking views from its huge suites overlooking the spectacular Nai Harn Bay and Promthep Cape. *$$$$*

Nai Yang

Pearl Village Resort
Nai Yang Beach
Tel: 0 7632 7006; Fax: 0 7632 7338
www.phuket.com/pearlvillage
Thai-style resort adjacent to a splendid beach fringed with pine trees that forms part of a national park. It is possible to take elephant rides on the beach, should you be feeling adventurous. The beautiful location is also very convenient for the airport. *$$$*

Pansea Beach

Amanpuri
Pansea Beach
Tel: 0 7632 4333; Fax: 0 7632 4014
www.amanpuri.com
In Sanskrit, *Amanpuri* means 'Place of Peace', a perfect description for this breathtaking resort located on isolated Pansea Beach. Part of the ultra-posh Amanresorts chain, the 70 Thai-style pavilions and villas have views either of the sea or lush gardens. Has won numerous international awards for its architecture and service.Easily the most expensive hotel in Phuket. *$$$$*

The Chedi Resort
118, Moo 3 Pansea Beach
Tel: 0 7632 4017/20; Fax: 0 7632 4252
www.ghmhotels.com
Isolated and elegant hillside resort of cottages linked by wooden walkways. Finding your room can sometimes be a nightmare as the walkways take a circuitous route to your cottage. Faces a fairly isolated white sand beach. Rooms are furnished simply with sundeck, queen-size beds, a safe and hairdryer. Known for its French-inspired seafood dining. *$$$$*

Patong

Amari Coral Beach Resort
2 Meun-ngem Road, South Patong
Tel: 0 7634 0106/14; Fax: 0 7634 0115
www.amari.com/coralbeach
Well-run remote hotel, located about 10 minutes' walk from the southern tip of Patong Beach. Trips to nearby Paradise Beach are popular with guests. First-rate Kinaree Thai and La Gritta Italian restaurants. Newly opened Sivara Spa offers a selection of spa treatments. *$$$*

Club Andaman Beach Resort
77/1 Thawiwong Road
Tel: 0 7634 0530; Fax: 0 7634 0527
www.clubandaman.com
Large hotel in expansive manicured gardens; close to, but not on the beach. Cottage accommodation in addition to hotel wing. Well-appointed rooms, with restaurants, pool, tennis courts and gym. *$$*

Diamond Cliff Resort
284 Prabaramee Road, Patong
Tel: 0 7634 0501/6; Fax: 0 7634 0507
www.diamondcliff.com/phuket
High-class resort catering to affluent Asian market, especially Japanese visitors. Located on a quiet corner at the north end of Patong Bay. Full facilities. *$$$*

Holiday Inn
52 Thawiwong Road
Tel: 0 7634 0608/9; Fax: 0 7634 0435
www.holidayinn.phuket.com
This is a popular resort hotel that attracts families who are on long vacations. Features a swimming pool and Pirate's Cove mini-golf for the children. Good steaks at Sam's Chicago Steak House. *$$$*

Impiana Phuket Cabana
41 Thawiwong Road
Tel: 0 7634 0138/40; Fax: 0 7634 0178
www.impiana.com
Medium-sized intimate resort located right by the sea in the centre of Phuket's busiest beach. Children's playground and pool with good water sports instructors and facilities. Very close to Patong Beach, shopping and nightlife. *$$$*

Patong Merlin
44 Thawiwong Road
Tel: 0 7634 0037/40; Fax: 0 7634 0394
www.merlinphuket.com
Large Thai-style hotel in south central Patong facing the beach. A busy hotel popular with Western holidaymakers. The Thai seafood restaurant is locally acclaimed. *$$*

Phuket Town

Metropole
Montri Road
Tel: 0 7621 5050; Fax: 0 7621 5990
www.metropolephuket.com
Modern and elegant high-rise hotel. Staff wear Thai traditional garb. Popular with business travellers as well as tourists. Very good food and beverage outlets, particularly the *Coffee Shop*'s buffet lunch. Simply put, a four-star hotel at three-star prices. *$$*

Pearl
42 Montri Road
Tel: 0 7621 1044; Fax: 0 7621 2911
e-mail: pearlhotel@phuket.com
Centrally located hotel popular with Asian tourists. Known for its Chinese rooftop restaurant, coffee shop, massage parlour and bowling alley. *$$*

Rawai

Evason Phuket Resort and Spa
100 Viset Road
Tel: 0 7638 1010/7; Fax: 0 7638 1018
www.sixsenses.com/evason-phuket
The only resort hotel in the southeast corner of the island. Guests have access to a free 20-minute boat shuttle to nearby Bon Island. The Six Senses Spa is the hotel's main draw. *$$$$*

Relax Bay (Karon Noi)

Le Meridien Phuket
29 Soi Karon Nui, Karon Noi Beach
Tel: 0 7634 0480/5; Fax: 0 7634 0479
www.lemeridien.com
Huge 470-room five-star hotel filled with activities all year round, including a glitzy variety show every night. Guests have access to what is effectively the hotel's own private beach, located in a small bay, midway between Patong and Karon. *$$$$*

Phi Phi Leh

Holiday Inn Resort
Laem Thong Beach
Tel: 0 7521 4654; Fax: 0 7521 5090
www.phiphi-palmbeach.com

Above: Le Meridien is the only hotel on Karon Noi Beach

Designer award-winning bungalows on isolated beach facing Bamboo and Mosquito 'desert' islands. Varied watersports, including scuba diving. *$$$*

PP Princess Diving & Spa Resort
Loh Dalam Bay
Tel: 0 7521 0928; Fax: 0 7521 7106
www.ppprincess.com
Comfortable beachfront bungalows with satellite TV and mini-bar. Faces Phi Phi's most attractive bay. Convenient walking distance to village. *$$*

Krabi Town
City Hotel
15/2 3 Sukon Road
Tel: 0 7562 1280
Clean and friendly family-run hotel with lovely touches like fruit basket and TV in each room. *$*

Maritime Park & Spa Resort
I Tungfah Road
Tel: 0 7562 0028/46; Fax: 0 7561 2992
www.krabi-hotels.com/maritime
Krabi Town's most luxurious hotel 2km (1 mile) from the town centre. Each room has a balcony overlooking limestone karsts, mangrove forests and the township. Satellite TV, coffee shop and swimming pool. *$$–$$$*

Viengthong Hotel
155/7 Uttarakit Road
Tel: 0 7562 0020

Centrally located hotel overlooking the river. Fan and air-conditioned rooms and a popular coffee shop open till late. *$*

Krabi Beaches – Ao Nang/Phra Nang
Gift's Bungalows
Ao Nang Beach Road
Tel: 0 7563 7166
Simple but clean jungle huts in a verdant tropical garden. Atmospheric restaurant serves tasty food and homemade breads. Surprisingly good for the price range. *$*

Phra Nang Inn
Ao Nang Beach Road
Tel: 0 7563 7130/3; Fax: 0 7563 7134
www.phrananginn.com
Conveniently located hotel fronting Ao Nang beach. Owners organise nature and culture tours. Has its own sea canoe facility for guests. Beachside restaurant and sunset bar. *$$*

Rayavadee
Phra Nang Headland
Tel: 0 7562 0740/2; Fax: 0 7562 0630
www.rayavadee.com
Stunning deluxe resort discreetly tucked away in the headland alongside Phra Nang and Rai Ley beaches. Attractive Thai-inspired two-storey bungalows are beautifully furnished and feature huge bathrooms. Watersports, tennis courts, sauna, gym. Three restaurants: Thai/seafood, international and light fare. *$$$$*

HEALTH AND EMERGENCIES

Hygiene/General Health

Drink only bottled water or soft drinks. Most hotels and large restaurants offer bottled water and clean ice. Thai chefs understand the importance of hygiene so the risk of food poisoning is quite small.

Stomach upsets are normally caused by over-indulgence. Most seafood is prepared hygienically but many foreigners overeat and their stomachs react negatively from a sudden switch to a cuisine radically different from the one they are used to.

Sunburn is also a problem; patients have been admitted with first and second-degree burns and swelling. The sun on a Phuket beach can do more damage in 1 hour than it can in 3 hours on a European beach. Apply sun block lotion generously.

With its thriving nightlife and transient population, Thailand is a magnet for sexually transmitted diseases. With AIDS on the rise, there is even more reason to be careful.

Medical Services

Pharmaceuticals ares of international standards, and pharmacies must be run by registered pharmacists. Most pharmacy personnel speak English. Some hotels in Patong have a doctor on call but for most medical problems you must go to a hospital or a clinic. Hospital Intensive Care units can generally handle emergencies quickly and competently. Most hospitals have foreign-trained doctors who can speak English. You should have no fears regarding medical treatment in the hospitals listed below. The privately run **Phuket International** and **Bangkok Phuket** hospitals (see below) generally have better facilities and service.

Phuket Town

Bangkok Phuket Hospital, 2/1 Honyok Utis Road, Phuket Town, tel: 0 7625 4425; **Mission Hospital**, Thepkasatri Road, tel: 0 7621 2386; **Phuket International Hospital**, Chalermprakiat Road, Phuket Town, tel: 0 7624 9400, fax: 0 7621 0936. For emergencies call tel: 0 7621 0935; **Phya Thai Phuket Hospital**, Sri Sena Road, Taladyai, tel: 0 7625 2603/6.

There are numerous medical clinics for minor ailments in Phuket Town. Staffed by licensed doctors, most are open until 10pm and even later. In Patong, there are several clinics along Soi Bangla. Inquire with the hotel desk for clinics in other locations.

Police

Regular police emergency hotline: tel: 191. Or you may prefer to call the Tourist Police on 1699. There is also a Tourist Service Line, tel: 1155, offering general advice.

COMMUNICATIONS AND NEWS

Post

General Post Office: 158 Montri Road, tel: 0 7621 1010 is open Mon–Fri 8.30am–4.30pm and Saturday 8.30am–noon. A *poste restante* service is also open during these hours and until 3.30pm on Saturday and Sunday. Phuket's *poste restante* post code is 83000. The **Patong Post Office**: junction of Thawiwong Road and Soi Post Office, near Siam Commercial Bank.

The **Tourism Authority of Thailand (TAT)** keeps incoming mail for tourists. Address it to (Name), c/o Tourism Authority of Thailand, 73–75 Phuket Road, Phuket Town, 83000, Thailand.

Telephone

The country code for Thailand is 66. Towns and cities within the country no longer have separate area codes, as the old area codes have been incorporated into local numbers. All phone numbers in Thailand now have eight digits. When calling inside Thailand, add a zero (eg: 0 7623 4451), but when calling from outside Thailand, no zero is necessary (eg: 66 7623 4451).

Overseas calls and faxes can be made at **Phuket Telecom Centre** (tel: 0 7621 6861) in Phang Nga Road in town. It is open 8am–midnight daily. Most hotels and also booths along the streets in Phuket, Patong, Kata and Karon offer long-distance telephone and fax services.

To call abroad directly, first dial the international access code 001, then the relevant country code: Australia (61); France (33);

Left: Ko Phi Phi's stunning coastal scenery

Germany (49); Italy (39); Japan (81); Netherlands (31); Spain (34); UK (44); US and Canada (1). For other countries, check wtih the hotel operator.

E-mails and Internet
You'll find plenty of cybercafés in Phuket, particularly in Phuket Town, Patong, Karon and Kata. Prices average around 40–50 baht per hour. Many hotels and guest-houses also offer Internet access, for double this price or more.

Media
The *Bangkok Post* and *The Nation* are among the best and most comprehensive English-language dailies in Asia. The *Asian Wall Street Journal* and the *International Herald Tribune*, and editions of British, French, German and Italian newspapers are available at major hotels. The locally produced weekly English-language newspaper, *Phuket Gazette,* is very informative.

Cable and satellite television is available in most major hotels.

USEFUL INFORMATION

Disabled
Facilities for the handicapped are under-developed although many of the top hotels do provide proper facilities. Few buildings in Phuket have wheelchair ramps.

Export Permits for Antiques
The Fine Arts Department prohibits the export of all Buddha images, deities and fragments (hands or heads) of images made prior to the 18th century.

Most of these items are found in northern and central Thailand, but if you do find one in Phuket, the shop can register it. Otherwise, take it to the Fine Arts Department in Bangkok on Na Prathat Road, together with two postcard-sized photos of it. The registration fee is between 50 and 200 baht.

Fake antiques or reproductions do not require export permits but Thai Airport Customs officials are not art experts and may mistake it for a genuine piece. If it looks authentic, clear it at the Fine Arts Department to avoid problems later.

Maps
Apart from the map included in the back of this book, there are a few commercially oriented ones available at hotel, tour and shop counters. These are the *A-O-A* and *Mag* freebie maps. The Tourism Authority of Thailand office in town gives away a useful light blue Phuket Town map.

Language
For centuries, the Thai language, rather than tripping from foreigners' tongues, has been tripping them up. Its roots go back to the place Thais originated from, in the hills of southern Asia – but is overlaid by Indian influences.

From the original settlers come the five tones, which seem designed to frustrate visitors – one sound with five different tones to mean five different things.

When you mispronounce, you don't simply say a word incorrectly, you say another word entirely. It is not unusual to see a semi-fluent foreigner standing before a Thai and running through the scale of tones until suddenly a light of recognition dawns on the listener's face.

There are misinformed individuals who will tell you that tones are not important. These people do not 'communicate' with Thais, they 'speak at' them in a one-sided exchange that frustrates both parties.

There is no universal transliteration system from Thai into English, which is why names and street names can be spelled several different ways.

Insight Guide: Thailand. Apa Publications, 13th edition, 2004, the companion guide to this book, has a comprehensive language section explaining the intricacies of the Thai language and its tonal system.

USEFUL ADDRESSES

Tourist Information
Tourism Authority of Thailand (TAT)
73–75 Phuket Road, Phuket Town
Tel: 0 7621 2213, 7621 1036
e-mail: tatphket@tat.or.th
www.tourismthailand.org
Has numerous brochures on accommodation, services and activities on the island.

Useful Websites

Websites worth surfing include following:
www.phuketinfo.com
www.phuketgazette.net
www.phuket.com
www.krabi-hotels.com
www.hotelthailand.com
www.thaihotels.org
www.thailandtravelguide.com

Airline Offices

Bangkok Airways, 158/2-3 Yaowaraj Road, tel: 0 7622 5033-5
China Airlines, Phuket International Airport, tel: 0 7632 7099
Dragonair, 156/14 Dhang Nga Road, tel: 0 7621 5734
Malaysian Airlines, 1/8-9 Thungkha Road, tel: 0 7621 6675
Phuket Air, 74/147 Poonphol Plaza, tel: 0 7622 0184
Silk Air, 183/103 Phang Nga Road, tel: 0 7621 3891
Singapore Airlines, 183/103 Phang-Nga Road, tel: 0 7621 3891
Thai Airways International (THAI), 78/1 Ranong Road, tel: 0 7621 2946

Travel Agents

Seatran Travel, 64/423 Mu 7 Anuphat Phuket Kan Road, tel: 0 7635 5410, e-mail: info@seatran.co.th
Siam Safari Nature Tours, 45 Chao Fa Road, Chalong, tel: 0 7628 0116, e-mail: info@siamsafari.com
Siam Exclusive Tours, 119 Rachauthit Road, Paradise Complex, Patong, tel: 0 7634 0912, e-mail: ewshkt@sun.phuket.ksc.co.th
Songserm Travel Center, 51 Satun Road, Phuket Town, tel: 0 7622 2570/4, e-mail: info@songsermtravel.com
Phuket Union Travel, 64/23 Chao Fa Road, Phuket Town, tel: 0 7622 5522, e-mail: info@phuketunion.com

FURTHER READING

Siam Mapped: A History of the Geo-Body of a Nation by Thongchai Winichakul, Honolulu: University of Hawaii Press, 1997. Comprises a thorough study of the development of Thai identity and sovereignty amid pressures from neighbouring South-East Asian kingdoms as well as European colonialism.

The Arts of Thailand by Steve Van Beek and Luca Tettoni, Periplus Editions, 1999 (revised edn). Lavishly illustrated, includes the minor arts.

Travelers' Tales Thailand ed by James O'Reilly and Larry Habegger, Travelers' Tales Guides, 2002. Essays on Thailand by noted travel writers such as Robert Sam Anson, Pico Iyer, Norman Lewis and William Warren.

Above: bumming on the beach

ACKNOWLEDGEMENTS

Cover	**Angelo Cavalli/Index Stock Imagery**
Backcover (top)	**Matthew Burns/Asia Images**
Backcover (bottom)	**Josef Beck**
Photography	**Steve Van Beek and**
Pages 55B	**Josef Beck**
32, 35, 43, 46B, 55T, 58, 72, 73	**Matthew Burns/Asia Images**
84	**Courtesy of Sheraton Grande Laguna**
34B, 59	**Oliver Hargreave/CPA**
14, 46T, 51, 63, 78	**David Henley/CPA**
12	**Hans Höfer**
25, 48, 49, 50	**Luca Invernizzi Tettoni/Photobank**
2/3, 20, 36B, 53, 61T/B, 62, 80	**Rainer Krack/CPA**
68	**Robin C. Nichols**
5, 54	**Photobank**
34T	**Larry Tackett**
6T/B, 7T/B, 8/9, 11, 23, 26T/B, 28, 29, 33, 40T, 42, 56, 64, 65, 67, 70, 74, 76, 82, 88, 91	**Marcus Wilson Smith/APA**
Cartography	**Maria Donnelly**
Cover Design	**Carlotta Junger**
Production	**Caroline Low**

© APA Publications GmbH & Co. Verlag KG Singapore Branch, Singapore

credits

INDEX